Mathematics
Projects
Handbook

Mathematics Projects Handbook

Fourth Edition

Glenn D. Allinger
Lyle E. Andersen
Cynthia S. Thomas
Karma G. Nelson
Adrien L. Hess

National Council of Teachers of Mathematics
Reston, Virginia

Copyright © 1977, 1982, 1989, 1999 by
THE NATIONAL COUNCIL OF TEACHERS OF MATHEMATICS, INC.
1906 Association Drive, Reston, VA 20191-1593

All rights reserved

Library of Congress Cataloging-in-Publication Data:

Mathematics projects handbook. — 4th ed. / Glenn D. Allinger ... [et al.]
      p.   cm.
    Rev. ed. of: Mathematics projects handbook. 3rd ed. / Adrien L. Hess, Glenn D. Allinger, Lyle E. Andersen. c1989.
    Includes bibliographical references.
    ISBN 0-87353-472-7
    1. Mathematics—Study and teaching (Middle school)
    2. Mathematics—Study and teaching (Secondary) I. Allinger, Glenn D. II. Hess, Adrien L. Mathematics projects handbook.
    III. National Council of Teachers of Mathematics.
    Qa11.M37584 1999
    510′.712—dc21   99-32453
                                     CIP

Printed in the United States of America

Contents

Dedications

The fourth edition of the *Mathematics Projects Handbook* is dedicated to **Adrien L. Hess** and **Glenn D. Allinger,** two longtime Montana mathematics educators. Between them, they have more than ninety years' experience teaching mathematics, working with teachers of mathematics, and serving as professional leaders in mathematics education at the local, state, and national levels. Hess was instrumental in establishing the Montana Council of Teachers of Mathematics (MCTM), and he served as its first president (1966–68). Allinger was instrumental in developing numerous statewide teacher professional development projects. Like Hess, his mentor and cohort, he served as the president of MCTM (1984–86).

Adrien L. Hess, 1908–1994

Adrien Hess, professor emeritus at Montana State University—Bozeman, wrote the first edition of the *Mathematics Projects Handbook* in 1977. During his fifty-five years of teaching, scholarship, and service at both the high school and college levels, he was constantly challenging students to excel in mathematics and science. That is one reason he served for twenty-four years as the director of the Montana Science Talent Search Program. This projects handbook was an effective outgrowth of his desire to teach about and sustain interest in the use of mathematics projects as an important learning experience for students. Adrien enthusiastically participated in two revisions (1982, 1989) of the handbook.

Glenn D. Allinger

Glenn Allinger, professor emeritus at Montana State University—Bozeman, was coauthor of the third and fourth editions of the *Mathematics Projects Handbook.* He received numerous outstanding teaching awards during his thirty-six year professional career, including being named Teacher of the Year (Senior High/University category) by MCTM in 1989. Glenn has always maintained a very keen interest in the professional development of teachers. He was selected as cochair of the Professional Development Committee in the National Science Foundation–funded Systemic Initiative for Montana Mathematics and Sciences (SIMMS) Integrated Mathematics Project (March 1991–September 1998). He enjoys challenging students and teachers to keep up with the changes occurring in mathematics education, and by following his example, to do their very best.

Other Authors

Lyle E. Andersen

Lyle Andersen, professor of mathematics education at Montana State University—Bozeman, was coauthor of the third and fourth editions of the *Mathematics Projects Handbook*. He has written numerous mathematics textbooks (grades K–12) and journal articles in mathematics education. He was the codirector of Montana's Systemic Teacher Excellence Preparation (STEP) project funded by NSF. He has a keen interest in integrating school mathematics and science through community-based research projects.

Cynthia S. Thomas

Cynthia Thomas taught for twenty-eight years at the elementary, middle school, and university levels. She is committed to the professional development of middle school, elementary, and preservice teachers. Cynthia is a recipient of the Presidential Award for Excellence in Science and Mathematics Teaching.

Karma G. Nelson

Karma Nelson has taught middle and high school mathematics for seventeen years and served as the District Secondary Math Specialist in Juneau, Alaska, for five years. She remains committed to improving mathematics education for all students by working with preservice and in-service teachers.

Introduction

MOST of us find great satisfaction in exhibiting the results of our study and labor and in comparing our efforts with those of others. Projects, fairs, and competitions in all areas of industry and art are familiar features in American life. Such experiences are pleasant and educational for all concerned: the exhibitor learns a great deal in preparing the exhibit, and the viewer learns something new from seeing it.

The project method of teaching was initiated more than sixty years ago by John F. Woodhull of Teachers College, Columbia University. It was described as a "normal, indeed ideal teaching process." Mathematics teachers have long valued the use of mathematical models and projects to arouse interest in mathematics. These ideas have gained momentum because of the growth of science fairs and the emphasis on mathematics stimulated by military and space-exploration rivalries and by advances in technology. Educators today also recognize the value of investigations and the importance of learning to use the Internet. Today, the uses of technology (graphing calculators, powerful PCs, data input devices, CD-ROMs, etc.) in the mathematics classroom offer wonderful opportunities for researching and displaying students' projects.

This handbook is designed as a guide for middle and high school teachers and students in choosing and developing mathematics projects. Those projects range from simple demonstrations of mathematical problems or principles that the teacher has assigned as classroom learning experiences to complex, sophisticated research projects intended for entrance in fairs and competitions.

The fourth edition of this handbook goes beyond simply updating references. Suggested resources take full advantage of the capabilities of Internet search machines and Web sites. New features include—

- new mathematics and statistics topics;
- expanded emphasis on middle school projects;
- tips on accessing and exploring Web sites;
- timelines and recording sheets for completion of projects;
- suggestions for collaboration of home, community and school;
- an ongoing Web site on Research in the Classroom with direct links to this Mathematics Projects Handbook.

(See www.math.montana.edu/~star/NCTMProjectBook. The World Wide Web [WWW] sites included in this handbook were operative at the time of publication at the addresses indicated. Some sites may have changed address, altered content, or may no longer exist. You are encouraged to add your own WWW sites.) Many positive things will happen in areas of learning and self-esteem when you bring investigation and research into your classroom. Just get started—good luck!

1

Developing a Mathematics Project

AMATHEMATICS project consists of all the effort expended in solving a problem, exploring an idea, researching a hypothesis, or applying a mathematical principle from beginning to end—that is, the initial planning, the study, the exhibit, and the written or audiovisual report.

The project could develop a new mathematical concept or theorem, show the relation of a mathematical idea or principle to some other branch of mathematics or science, or demonstrate the application of a mathematical idea or principle. It might be an investigation using a symbolic manipulator (e.g., *Mathematica*), or exploring conjectures with a geometric manipulator (e.g., *Geometric superSupposer*) where the student is discovering an original theorem. In this type of project the student is looking for a mathematical relationship to be explored deductively. The power of exploring mathematics with the capabilities of technology can be very exciting.

The exhibit uses drawings, graphs, models, pictures, words, and so on, to tell the viewer briefly the student's idea of the mathematical concept or the scientific finding and to show its use in explaining some biological or physical phenomenon. Thus the project is the whole process, whereas the exhibit is the tangible attempt to show and explain the project to anyone who is interested.

TYPES OF PROJECTS

Projects are usually of three general types. They are: (1) **documentation projects,** which involve finding out information about a subject, a person, or a discovery made by someone else and reporting on the findings; (2) **documentation/experimentation projects,** which go beyond documentation and include the answering of a question or proving of a conjecture or hypothesis; and (3) **experimentation projects,** which involve conducting, analyzing, and reporting on a carefully controlled, inductive experiment or the development of a deductive proof.

Documentation projects are important learning experiences for students because they can involve searching for information, but they normally involve only lower-level reasoning. Experimentation projects usually involve higher-level reasoning and create learning environments that encourage students' understanding of the scientific endeavor.

Choosing a Project

The best projects grow out of students' interests; therefore, they should be chosen by the students themselves. The selected projects should express the students' broadest knowledge and highest skills, and they should be enjoyable to do. Teachers' suggestions, mathematics club meetings, demonstrations, lists of previous projects, and so on help stimulate students' interest. Today's advances in technology have created numerous new opportunities that students can use when looking for projects. Searching the World Wide Web (WWW), an important contemporary learning tool, might lead to exciting opportunities involving topics such as space travel or newly created mathematics (i.e., dynamical systems and chaos theory), which may be applied to real-world problems. Mathematical power, not previously available to students, can now be used by students who work with high-level calculators (i.e., the Texas Instruments TI-92) or a high-speed computer. Chapter 3 gives some titles of previous projects and suggestions for others.

Students should be encouraged to use technology when creating their presentations. Software such as PowerPoint and EXCEL are excellent choices because they provide tools for the students to create outstanding exhibits.

RESEARCH METHODS

Once a specific idea or problem has been chosen, it should be thought through carefully. The successive steps should be enumerated and possible pitfalls noted. A written record should be kept at every stage of the project. (See Appendix C.)

When the preliminary plans are made, the student should begin a comprehensive reading program to broaden his or her understanding of the possibilities and limitations of the proposed project. Extensive use should be made of WWW searches, books, and periodicals from all available sources.

Since accurate notes should be kept of all readings, observations, suggestions, and speculations, paper and pencil or a computer should be handy at all times. The notes should include a complete record of sources. Examples are shown below.

National Council of Teachers of Mathematics Web site www.nctm.org/publications

Organization name   Site address   Subcategory

Author   *Title*

Malloy, Carol E. "Mathematics Projects Promote Students' Algebraic Thinking." *Mathematics Teaching in the Middle School* 2 (February 1997): 282–88.

           Journal   **Volume**   **Date**   **Pages**

Farmer, David W., and Theodore B. Stanford. *Knots and Surfaces: A Guide to Discovering Mathematics*. Washington, D.C.: American Mathematical Society, 1996.

The selection of a topic or idea to explore is difficult and all-important. Students should be encouraged to look for ideas that require higher-order thinking. Ideas found during the search should be recorded even if they seem irrelevant at the time. Often, new ideas can be better evaluated after they have "simmered" for a while.

As the exploration of the topic develops, plans can be discussed with other people. Discussing an idea with someone else often gives a new and clearer perspective. Parents, teachers, professional mathematicians, scientists and engineers, community professionals, and other students can often make constructive comments, criticisms, or suggestions.

In all research, experimentation, and study, the student should keep in mind the last step in the preparation of the exhibit—the completion of the written report (Gerver [50]). If all ideas (original or not), guesses (good or bad), measurements, sketches, and readings are recorded in the notebook as the project develops, the final report will be much easier to write. Specific guidelines are available for competitions. The final report, however, will include the following:

- Title
  Project name, student's name, school, grade

- Statement of the Problem or Investigation
  The essentials of the investigation or research must be clearly stated.

- Table of Contents
  List each component of the paper and the page number where it begins. The table of contents is completed after everything else is done and the pages are numbered.

- Introduction
  One paragraph that gives an overview of the project. This paragraph should give the reader a brief synopsis of the project. It contains the hypothesis and an explanation of why the student chose this topic and what he or she hoped to find or prove.

- Background research
  Include what was found in the published materials. Use popular sources such as newspapers and magazines as well as WWW sites, books, scientific journals, technical materials, and interviews.

- Procedure

  The procedure, methods, and materials for investigation or experiment may be communicated as lists or written in paragraph form. Drawings may help make the information more clear. Tell exactly what was done. Show all the information found, including the steps that initially led to errors.

- Results

  What are the findings? Are the results consistent with commonly held beliefs? Briefly summarize the results. Be specific. Do not generalize.

  Documentation projects need to show clearly what the investigator was looking for, what was found, and what important concepts, ideas, and conclusions were reached.

  Documentation/experimentation projects include documentation and a careful description of the experiment and results.

  Experimentation projects involve conducting, analyzing, and reporting on a carefully controlled, inductive experiment or the development of a deductive proof. Experimentation projects should contain tables and graphs that communicate the findings and show the extent to which the data supports the research hypothesis.

- Extensions

  List any new research ideas that this project suggested. Investigations often raise more questions than are answered.

  After the exhibit and the written report are completed, the student should consider what questions the judges or interested spectators might ask. (See Evaluation Criteria [Form 1] in this chapter and Evaluation Criteria [Form 2] in Appendix A). The student should be able to explain the project both to the judges, who may be experts in the field, and to a layperson, who may be interested but not well informed about the subject.

CONSTRUCTION MATERIALS AND METHODS

Selecting and using materials is an important factor in the success of an exhibit. For a project that requires a computer, a great amount of the software is already available, and an electronic presentation (e.g., PowerPoint audiovisual computer-assisted presentation) would likely enhance the project. Developing a mathematical model that provides an explanation of the mathematics is strongly encouraged. The exhibit must be designed with several things in mind. From the standpoint of its maker, the exhibit should be—

- *functional:* It should tell the story of the study and research, and any displayed material should be in harmony with this objective;
- *practical:* The number of components, the time needed to set them up, and any limits on the contents of the exhibits must be considered;
- *portable:* The exhibit should be compact, durable, and easy to transport.

RESPONSIBILITIES AND GUIDANCE

Preparing a mathematics project can be an interesting and worthwhile experience. Students will get experience in using resources to find information, in doing independent work, in organizing their presentations, and in communicating ideas orally, visually, and in writing. They will broaden their backgrounds in mathematics and explore mathematical topics they never knew existed. In setting up exhibits, they will experience the satisfaction of demonstrating what they have accomplished. Students will grow in self-confidence as they share their experiences with one another. They may satisfy their curiosity and their desire to be creative. They may develop originality, craftsmanship, and new mathematical understanding. Preparing the project can help them experience the beauty and functionality of mathematics. As a result, they may decide to make mathematics their career. At the same time, the project will dramatize the nature of mathematics to students, teachers, and citizens of the community.

The Responsibility of the Student

In organizing a successful exhibit, students will find the following suggestions helpful:

1. *Select a topic that has high interest potential.* The areas mentioned in chapter 2 and specific topics listed in chapter 3 suggest many possibilities.

2. *Find as much information about the topic as possible.* Check WWW sites, books, journals, and cumulative indexes (e.g., Education Research Information Center [ERIC], which is also online [ericir.syr.edu]). Chapters 4 and 5 include several suggestions.

3. *Prepare and organize the material into a concise, interesting report.* Include color drawings, pictures, applications, and examples that will capture the reader's attention and add meaning to the exhibit.

4. *Build an exhibit that will tell the story of the topic.* Exhibits are usually judged on the following criteria: creative ability, mathematical thought, thoroughness, skill, and clarity. Use models, applications, or charts that lend

variety. If possible, prepare materials that viewers can manipulate. Give the exhibit a catchy, descriptive title. Label everything with brief captions or legends so that viewers will understand the principles involved. Make the display simple but also attractive and dramatic. Do not try to say too much. Have a one-page summary of the basic ideas, plans, and important references available for distribution.

5. *Be able to demonstrate the topics of the exhibit.* Speak clearly and correctly. Be well informed in order to answer questions. Be appropriately dressed, courteous, and congenial to the viewers as well as the judges.

The Role of the Mathematics Teacher

One of the most important functions of the mathematics teacher is to provide enthusiasm and inspiration so that students will *want* to do a project. The teacher needs to provide a wide selection of ideas and suggestions that will be suitable for mathematics projects. (See chapters 2 and 3.) Examples of previous projects, if available, are helpful. With the help of the school librarian and directed Internet investigations, the teacher can provide a well-rounded selection of Internet sources, books, periodicals, and pamphlets on mathematics.

The teacher needs to be ready to help the student choose a project and should review the criteria for it before the work actually begins. The project should interest the student greatly and be within the student's mathematical ability.

The teacher need not be an expert in the subject the student chooses. It is important that the teacher offer guidance throughout the preparation of the exhibit and maintain a cheerful and optimistic attitude at all times, especially when the student is not making the progress she or he desires.

Project progress reports need to be made by each participant. The report must include an updated timeline for completing the project. (See Appendix C for a project progress report form that can be duplicated.)

Finally, the teacher should check the finished exhibit and project report for the correct use of mathematical principles and terms and for accuracy in grammar and spelling.

The Role of the Evaluators

The people who take time to evaluate projects do so because they are interested in young investigators and in mathematics. Ideally, the evaluating should be divided into four steps.

1. Evaluators should initially assess each exhibit independently on the basis of criteria given to the students. During this examination they may take notes regarding questions to ask, points to discuss, and improvements to suggest to the exhibitor.

2. After this preliminary examination, the exhibitor should be interviewed. The purpose of this activity is to ascertain what the exhibitor has really learned. Students should be informed ahead of time that this will happen. The interview is one phase of the learning process and should not be omitted. Evaluators should be ready and willing to give suggestions and ideas to the exhibitor.

3. In the final stage, the evaluation results should be examined by the evaluators, and the individual ratings can be discussed if they wish.

4. Evaluation results should be shared with exhibitors in written form. If the results are to be made public, the format and method of publication should be clearly stated in information provided prior to the fair.

EVALUATION CRITERIA

It is helpful to have certain criteria and standards to use as a guide in evaluating projects. One such guide for mathematics projects follows. The categories and descriptions have been modified from the "Judging Guidelines & Evaluation Criteria," a tool of the Intel International Science and Engineering Fair (ISEF). (The Intel ISEF is purported to be the "Olympics, the World Series, and the World Cup of science [and mathematics] competitions." The contest brings together students, teachers, corporate executives, and government officials around the world. Science Service, a nonprofit organization based in Washington, D.C., has administered the ISEF since its inception in 1950. For further information, access Web site www.sciserv.org/iisef.htm.)

Evaluation Criteria (Form 1)

Project Title _____

Project Creator _____

I. Creative Ability (30 points)
   1. Does the project show creative ability and originality in—
      • approach to solving the problem?
      • collection and analysis of data?
      • use of existing tools?
      • design of new tools?
   2. Does the project answer a question in an original way?

II. Mathematical Thought (30 points)
   1. Is the problem stated clearly?
   2. Is the problem sufficiently limited?
   3. Are all aspects of the problem clearly recognized and defined?
   4. Are there adequate data to support the conclusions?
   5. Does the student understand the project's ties to related research?
   6. Does the student have an idea of what further research is warranted?
   7. Is the conclusion accurate?
   8. Is the conclusion significantly different from previous alternatives?
   9. Did the student perform all the mathematical thinking, or did someone help?

III. Thoroughness (15 points)
   1. How completely was the problem or topic covered?
   2. How complete are the notes?
   3. Is the student aware of other approaches or theories?
   4. Is the student familiar with scientific literature in the studied field?
   5. How much time did the student spend on the project?

IV. Skill (15 points)
   1. Does the student have the skills required to collect the data?
   2. What equipment was used? Did the student build it?
   3. Was the exhibit completed with adult assistance or supervision? Who and how much?

V. Clarity (10 points)

1. How clearly does the student discuss the project, including purpose, procedure, and conclusions?

2. Does the student have a memorized speech that reflects little understanding?

3. Does the written material reflect the student's understanding of the research?

4. Are the data presented clearly?

5. Are the results presented clearly?

6. How well does the display explain the project?

7. Was the presentation done in a forthright manner?

AFTER THE EXHIBIT

A student who has one or more years remaining in middle school or high school may want to continue working on the exhibit the following year. It often takes more than one year to produce an outstanding exhibit. Senior students may wish to donate their exhibits to the mathematics department. Mathematics teachers in the local school should encourage students with exemplary projects to make presentations in mathematics classrooms. Such role models can influence both younger and older students.

Service clubs and parent-teacher groups are usually willing to have a student discuss his or her exhibit at one of their meetings. The student not only gains experience in discussing the project but informs the public of school activities as well.

If the written report is of sufficient interest, some variation of it can be submitted by the participant and teacher for publication in professional journals such as the *Mathematics Teacher* or *Mathematics Teaching in the Middle School*. See chapter 4 for a list of other periodicals.

General Topics

THE following topics provide examples of subjects through which a particular project can be chosen and developed. Each topic is discussed briefly. Suggestions and questions are given to stimulate further thought and study on some particular aspect. A brief list of selected resources is included under each topic. (See chapter 5 for full bibliographical information on these resources.)

It is important that students choose topics that they are interested in and that are not too general. For example, "number systems" is too large. Also, interest is much more likely to remain high if the student can experiment with the topic in some type of inquiry mode rather than simply documenting a topic that someone else discovered or created. "Create a base 12, twelve-month calendar" could be a good experimentation study. If the student plans to study "How computers work" by taking one apart, then he or she is preparing a documentation study. Using a computer software package to "Compare the areas of the polygons formed by connecting the midpoints of the sides of a regular polygon" could be a good experimental topic. The preceding examples show the difference between experimentation and documentation. Documentations may be appropriate as class projects; however, for regional, state, or national mathematics and science competitions (e.g., Intel International Science and Engineering Fair), students will have to choose a topic and narrow it to a specific question or a problem that allows for experimentation.

GRADES 6–8

Calculating Instruments, Measuring Devices, and Computing Methods

The construction and use of calculating instruments and measuring devices is important and worthwhile. However, the mathematical principles being modeled by the device or instruments are even more important. If the student can apply the principle to a new situation or put a measuring device to a new use, the result becomes even more worthwhile. Devices and instruments such as the soroban, the abacus, the slide rule, and Napier's rods or bones can serve as mathematical models, provide interesting histories about the development of computation tools, and be used in project applications. Some commonly used tools such as the compass, ruler, Vernier calipers, and protractor also have fascinating histories. Interesting projects can also be developed by learning about the inventor and how the invention was used. John Napier's bones or rods provide us with an excellent example. The student could also find other mathematical devices invented by Napier.

- Are Napier's rods still commonly used?
- Where is the abacus still used?
- Is the calculator faster than the abacus?

Students are often intrigued by calculation methods that vary from traditional algorithms. A student might develop a project on alternative algorithms for division.

- Why do the scratch, doubling and summing, and lattice methods of multiplication work?
- What are the "Russian peasant" and the "finger method" for multiplication? Why do they work?
- What contributions did Babbitt, Von Neumann, Kemeny, and Papert make with regard to computers?
- What is the Greenwood method of division?
- How do computers work?

The following are selected references on these topics. The number in parentheses refers to the number of the reference entry in chapter 5.

Gardner (44)	Good (183)	Karp (197)
Lappan (84)	Lamb (200)	
Perry (217)	Wolfram (159)	

sln.fi.edu/tfi/hotlists/math.html	

(Record your favorite Web sites here.)

Numeration Systems

Numeration systems are a fertile source of topics for projects. The rudiments of many of the ideas may already be familiar to the students, but the theory behind them and their applications may intrigue them.

A number is a concept or an idea. That idea can be expressed as a numeral using different kinds of symbols. Numerous number systems have been developed through the ages (i.e., Roman numerals, the Egyptian numeration system, and cuneiform are a few examples). The Hindu-Arabic number system that we use originated about A.D. 600.

- What are some ancient methods of recording results of counting?
- What is the Euclid algorithm?
- How are Morse code, Braille, semaphore, and sign language related to numbers, numerals, and number systems?
- Can you create your own number system?
- What is a symmetric numeration system?

Arcavi (163)	Kliman (199)
Bendick (10)	Michalowicz (211)
Hughes (191)	

(Record your favorite Web sites here.)

Number Bases

Number bases other than base ten are valuable for students to investigate. Students can create addition and multiplication tables and learn about the field properties for a number system. The basis for all digital computers is electronic circuits that have only two states—either on or off—which correspond to the binary (base two) numbers one and zero. Even computers that use a hexidecimal system (base sixteen) are extensions of the binary principle.

- Can negative numbers be used for bases?
- Can fractions be used with bases other than base ten (e.g., base two)?
- Can base-ten calculating devices and strategies be used with other number bases?
- What base systems are used in Nim or in a set of cards to tell a person's age?
- Can you build a base-twelve calendar?

Karp (197)

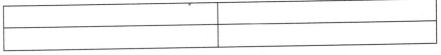

(Record your favorite Web sites here.)

Sets

The notion of sets, or collections of objects, is nearly as ancient as the human race. It was not until the late nineteenth century that mathematicians concluded that sets are an important basic mathematical concept.

- What are sets, and how can they be applied to number systems and operations on number systems (arithmetic)?
- How are set theory and electric circuitry related?
- How do the prime numbers relate to the Fibonacci numbers?
- How is set notation used in geometry?
- How are Venn diagrams used to solve problems?

Bennett (167)   ·   Quesada (221)
Lauber (201)

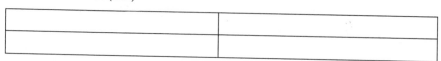

(Record your favorite Web sites here.)

Statistics and Probability

All biological and physical phenomena lend themselves to data collection and the subsequent application of statistics. A study involving one or both of these concepts can be somewhat elementary, or it can be quite complex and extend over several years. Data used in statistics must be obtained by measuring, recording, or weighing various objects and phenomena.

Students could develop a survey, use the survey to create a prediction instrument, and represent the results with statistical representations (e.g., histograms, graphs, etc.). Students could also use and interpret statistical procedures such as scatterplots, box-and-whisker plots, and stem-and-leaf plots to represent their data. Investigations, which include carefully designed experiments, will help students see practical uses and possible misuses of statistics.

- Are measures of central tendency equivalent?
- What are measures of dispersion?
- Into what kind of statistical pattern do errors of measurement fall?
- Why are random numbers useful when simulating the likelihood of events?
- Why are lines useful on scatterplots?
- What does the Law of Large Numbers imply about flipping a coin?

The unit project "The Carnival Game" in *What Do You Expect?* (The Connected Mathematics Project [84]) provides an excellent example of scoring guides for students' work on the project.

Burrill (18)
Johnson (195)
Kader (196)
Landwehr (82)
Lappan (84)
May (209)

Newman (99)
Perry (217)
Uccellini (233)
VanLeuvan (234)
Wilson (238)
Zawojewski (161)

www.learner.org/cgi-bin/w3-msql/exhibits/statistics/activity0/frontpoll	

(Record your favorite Web sites here.)

Paper Folding

Paper folding can be effectively used to develop or extend a project in mathematics at the middle school level. Paper folding and creasing can be used, with certain assumptions, to create any construction that can be made with traditional tools. The construction of regular polygons with strips of paper is intriguing. The method of building a "hexaflexagon" can be shown to unify algebra and geometry. This method can also be used to find the area of a triangle.

- What assumptions are made when paper folding is used to construct geometric figures?
- What polygons and polyhedrons can be made by paper folding?
- How can paper folding be used to show certain mathematical fallacies?
- How can paper folding be extended to knot theory?
- How can some conjectures be proved with the help of paper-folding techniques?

Geometer's Sketchpad (240)
Johnson (72)
Sierra (131)

www.lwcd.com/paper-folding	
www.lwcd.com/paper-folding/geometry.html	

(Record your favorite Web sites here.)

Curve Stitching

Students are initially amazed to see that curves can be constructed with a series of line segments by using a straightedge, paper folding, string, or geometry visualization software. Curve stitching can also lead students to the concepts of calculus and limits. For example, a line representing a function can be thought of as a collection of very short line segments, and the area under a curve can be pictured as a sum of rectangles that are infinitesimally narrow.

- How can curves be formed by straight lines?
- Can curve stitching be used to make three-dimensional models of curves?
- What is the envelope of a curve?
- How do aborigines of Australia, Navajos and Eskimos of North America, and Batwa pygmies of Africa use string art in their cultures?

Pohl (109)   Whatley (155)

(Record your favorite Web sites here.)

Optical Illusions

Seeing is believing, but sometimes our eyes deceive us! Some illusions have more than one explanation. As research and experiments are done, ideas about optical illusions change. Students will discover that optical illusions are used in many ways. Illusions are an essential tool in some types of artwork. (See the Patterns and Art section on p. 21.) Special mirrors can produce optical illusions that make us laugh. Occasionally, illusions lead us to erroneous conjectures.

- Why do patterns cause illusions?
- Can optical illusions be extended to three dimensions?
- What tricks depend on optical illusions?
- How are optical illusions used in camouflaging, advertising, dress design, and architecture?
- Can you create "magic" using optical illusions?

Ernst (34)

www.WorldOfEscher.com	
www.lainet.com/~ausbourn/links.html	

Motion Geometry

Many people believe that the most useful everyday geometry involves slides, flips, turns, and combinations of these moves. In 1872 Felix Klein, a twenty-three-year-old professor at the University of Erlangen, defined geometry as the study of properties of figures that do not change when a figure is transformed. This geometry is called motion or transformation geometry.

- What are some everyday examples of motion geometry?
- How can motions be duplicated using the compass, straightedge, or paper tracing?
- How can the computer language called Logo and the movement of the turtle teach us about motions?
- How does a kaleidoscope use motion or transformation geometry?
- Can you create a four-line geometry?

Bidwell (168)	TesselMania! (242)
Seymour (124)	Woodward (160)

www.WorldOfEscher.com	www.ScienceU.com

(Record your favorite Web sites here.)

Geometry

Ancient Babylonians used geometric principles to measure land areas. This is reflected in the name *geometry,* which literally means "land measure." The study of geometric shapes and their properties is an essential component of mathematics that is rich in concepts and applications. The importance of geometry goes well beyond its everyday uses or even its many applications in architecture, engineering, and design. An understanding and appreciation of geometry is basic to understanding and appreciating mathematics.

- What are projective, descriptive, and differential geometries and how are they similar and different?
- Which regular *n*-gons tessellate the plane? Why?
- Why does Pick's Theorem work?
- Why are isoperimetric figures interesting?
- How can geometry be used to measure distance indirectly?

Discovering geometric theorems intuitively by using a calculator or computer geometry software package (e.g., Geometer's Sketchpad) has tremendous potential.

- What do you notice about the areas of the four small triangles that result when you connect the midpoints of the sides of a triangle?
- What is the sum of the interior angles of a triangle, quadrilateral, decagon, ..., n-gon? Prove your conjecture.

Fragale (181)	Naraine (214)
Geddes (49)	Pollack (219)
Geometer's Sketchpad (240)	Seymour (123)
Geometric superSupposer (241)	Slavit (230)
Greeley (185)	Smart (133)
Laycock (86)	Thomas (147)
Markowitz (210)	Whatley (155)
Millman (212)	

forum.swarthmore.edu/dr.math/faq/faq.impossible.construct.html

(Record your favorite Web sites here.)

Functions

A function is a basic concept. It is useful to describe it in several ways, including a collection of ordered pairs, points on a two-dimensional graph, or a specific formula stating a relationship.

- How is a piecewise function determined?
- Can all functions be represented with a diagram or a model?
- Are all relations functions?
- How did Galileo define functions for physical sciences?
- What can be expected if a nonlinear function is iterated so that the value for every iteration is included sequentially in the next one?
- Given a set of data points on a plane, can you find a function that contains every data point?

Andreasen (162)	Phillips (107)
Coes (174)	Rubenstein (223)
Malloy (207)	Stacey (231)
Patterson (216)	

(Record your favorite Web sites here.)

Patterns and Art

One of the earliest mathematical structures that students explore is patterning, usually through sounds and geometric shapes. That structure is extremely valuable when extending patterning to algebraic thinking. Mathematics is sometimes referred to as the science of patterns. Patterns in mathematics extend naturally into discussions and explorations of patterns in art and nature. The works of M. C. Escher can foster curiosity for many students. One example of patterning is the classic handshake problem. Patterning extends to symmetry and a rich source of projects can be found in the symmetry of chaos.

- What patterns are found in common algebraic manipulations?
- Analyze the wall patterns found in the Alhambra.
- How do the legal moves in a 15-puzzle correspond to permutations?
- How do Native American star quilts, Amish quilts, and West African Kente cloth compare?
- What are the figurate numbers, and how do they relate to dot patterns?

Andreasen (162)	Lemon (202)
Austin (164)	Malloy (207)
Curcio (176)	TesselMania! (241)
Devlin (33)	Walton (236)
Field (40)	

www.ece.ucdavis.edu/~hardaker/escher	
www.WorldOfEscher.com	www.tessellations.com

(Record your favorite Web sites here.)

Games and Puzzles

Games have played a significant and colorful role in human history. Some of the oldest recorded games have been found on Egyptian tombs. Puzzles can be used to arouse students' interest in mathematical activities and encourage creative approaches to problem solving.

- What methods and strategies are used in games throughout the world?
- At what point do you know that you have won a game?
- Is there an advantage to being the first or last player?
- Can you develop a winning strategy for ticktacktoe? Other games?

Gardner (44, 45, 46)   Sharp (128)
Gorman (184)   Stewart (144)
Pappas (102)

(Record your favorite Web sites here.)

Calendar and Time

Most students will be surprised to discover that all calendars do not look like the ones Americans use. An investigation into various historical calendars will include an investigation into the development of numbers.

- Why isn't our calendar divided into months with equal numbers of days?
- How did Pope Gregory XIII solve the leap-year problem?
- How did Babylonians, Romans, and Egyptians keep track of days?
- How do African calendars compare?
- Are apparent solar time, mean solar time, and sidereal time equal?

Bennett (167)
Burns (16)
Shirley (228)

(Record your favorite Web sites here.)

Topology, Knots, and Surfaces

The study of topology is explorations into properties of geometric figures that are stretched, shrunk, twisted, or somehow distorted. Topology has been described as "rubber-sheet" geometry. Investigations into graph diagrams and knots and their surfaces will lead to very interesting projects. In 1736 Leonard Euler used circuit tracing to solve the Königsberg Bridge problem, which had intrigued mathematicians for years. His methods of circuit tracing are used today in many mathematical explorations.

- What is a Möbius strip, a Klein bottle, a Jordan curve?
- How could the letters of the alphabet be sorted with respect to topology?
- What is the four-color theorem?
- How are maps and graph diagrams related?

- Does Euler's formula hold for any connected graph drawn on a sphere?

Barnes (165)	Lappan (84)
Farmer (38)	Naraine (214)

www.cs.uidaho.edu/~casey931/new_knot/index.html	

(Record your favorite Web sites here.)

Algebra

Algebra includes five components: mathematical language; patterns, relations, and functions; multiple representations; modeling; and structure. These components share equal importance in the middle school. Mathematical language includes the use of variables and symbols. The concept of a function develops as one of the most important ideas as students learn to work with generalizations. A problem can be represented numerically, graphically, and symbolically. Mathematical modeling helps students make connections to real-world situations and includes concrete materials such as charts, tables, and simulations. Organizing algebra as a structure means that students think about how number systems are built from axioms such as the associative property.

- Are leveling payments cost effective?
- How do the length of a side and the area of a square relate?
- Analyze the resiliency of a ball's bounce.
- How can algebra be used to perform a mathematics trick?
- How fast can a group of people holding hands pass a squeeze?
- How can problems involving functions be solved numerically, graphically, and symbolically?

Austin (164)	NCTM (95)
Johnson (195)	Patterson (216)
Jones (73)	Stacey (231)
Malloy (207)	

(Record your favorite Web sites here.)

The Golden Section

If a line segment is divided into two segments so that one section is the mean proportional between the whole line segment and the other segment, the line is said to be divided into extreme and mean ratios. The Greeks considered this proportion to have mystical significance and called it the *divine proportion*. Today it is known as the *golden section*. A rectangle formed by using the longer part of the golden section as its length and the shorter part as its width is considered to have the most eye-pleasing proportions that can be found in nature. This construction is used in inscribing a regular decagon in a given circle.

- How is the Fibonacci sequence related to the golden section?
- What relationship does the Fibonacci sequence have to the plant world? The animal world?
- Do any of the Platonic solids exemplify the golden section?
- Are Pascal's triangle and the golden ratio related?
- How is the golden ratio used in art work?

> Garland (47)
>
> Manuel (208)
>
> Schwartzman (226)

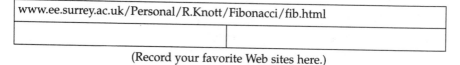

www.ee.surrey.ac.uk/Personal/R.Knott/Fibonacci/fib.html	

(Record your favorite Web sites here.)

Discrete Mathematics

Discrete mathematics deals with the arrangements of discrete objects. For example, directed graphs, not to be confused with the graph of a function, are often used. They are collections of vertices with edges connecting some of them. Directed means the edges have arrows on them. Discrete mathematics offers a wealth of other challenging possibilities. Topics included are inductive and deductive reasoning, recursion, combinations and permutations, and logic and puzzles. Software tools such as Logo, TesselMania!, and Geometer's Sketchpad can be especially helpful for students in many of their explorations.

- How can election districts be apportioned fairly?

- How does discrete math play a part in doctors' decisions on the timing and size of dosages of medicine?
- Can a shortest route to any given five cities be found?
- Can you write a program that constructs Sierpinski's triangle on a graphing calculator?
- Can you use a directed graph to solve a complicated scheduling problem?

Crisler (27)	Rosenstein (116)
Geometer's Sketchpad (240)	Seymour (127)
Kenney (75)	TesselMania! (242)

(Record your favorite Web sites here.)

Group Theory

A group is one of the simplest and most important mathematical systems. The concept of groups is fundamental to crystallography, cryptanalysis, and quantum mechanics. Models depicting groups of movements for triangles, circles, and squares can easily be constructed and generated using three-dimensional objects. Applications can also be made to elementary trigonometry.

- How does the algebraic concept of groups help unify different branches of mathematics?
- Does knot theory have a relationship to group theory?
- Does modular arithmetic have a connection with groups?
- Do certain Boolean algebras that form a group under specified operations have a connection?
- How do groups show relationships between geometry and modern abstract algebra?

Copes (23)
Farmer (37)
Shifrin (130)

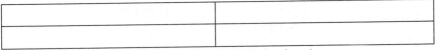

(Record your favorite Web sites here.)

Binomial Theorem

The binomial theorem has many applications, including computing compound interest and depreciation and approximating the roots of numbers. The binomial expansion theorem can be generalized by students using an symbolic manipulator to find $(a + b)^0$, $(a + b)^1$, $(a + b)^2$, $(a + b)^3$....

- How can Pascal's triangle be used in binomial expansion?
- How does the binomial theorem apply to such diverse phenomena as the growth of timber, the increase of bacteria, the surface healing of wounds, the decomposition of radium, or the loss of heat or electrical energy?
- How does statistics use the binomial model?
- Can the binomial theorem be used in studying blood types or Mendel's laws?
- What theorem dealing with complex numbers uses the binomial theorem?
- What is the connection between combinations and the binomial theorem?

  Courant (24)
  Cuff (175)
  Tucker (149)

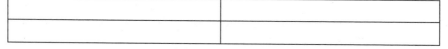

(Record your favorite Web sites here.)

Technology

Computers

Technology has spurred a growth of interest in mathematics by encouraging the rapid application of mathematics to science. As a result of technology, existing fields of mathematics and science have been reexamined and new fields created. Changes are so rapid that to keep abreast of the current status of both hardware and software, constant use must be made of periodicals and the Internet.

- What mathematical subjects have become important with the advent of computers? Less important?
- What new mathematics subjects have been generated using the computer as a tool?
- Can the computer learn or create mathematics?

- How is the computer used to aid in the solution of some of the unsolved problems in mathematics?
- How are the ideas of set theory, topology, and symbolic logic applied to computers?
- Why has the computer increased the use of probability as a very significant tool for simulation and modeling?
- How can a computer be used to generate conjectures that might eventually be proved as theorems?

Bennett (11)	McGehee (206)
Chhatwal (20)	Peitgen (105)
Gnanadesikan (51)	Schimmel (225)
Heid (58)	Shilgalis (227)
Holden (189)	St. John (232)
Kimberling (198)	Williams (158)
Lovinelli (203)	Wolfram (159)

(Record your favorite Web sites here.)

Graphing Calculators

Relatively inexpensive graphing calculators have become daily tools in most secondary school mathematics classrooms. They have expanded the possibilities of simulating mathematical phenomena for younger students. The graphing calculator combined with the Calculator Based Laboratory (CBL) enables students to collect natural data using a variety of probes and then transfer that data to a graphing calculator for graphical analysis.

- What process does the calculator use to compute a regression equation to model a data set?
- What are the effects of rounding off or truncating on computations carried out with a calculator?
- Investigate a problem such as compound interest using the iterative process with a calculator.
- Use a graphing calculator to develop a conjecture and investigate it further.

Brueningsen (15)	Vonder Embse (235)
Johnson (194)	Williams, D. E. (157)
MCTM/SIMMS (90)	Williams, M. R. (158)
St. John (232)	

www.ti.com/calc/docs/graphs.htm	

(Record your favorite Web sites here.)

Geometries

"Geometry must be approached from multiple perspectives to permit the user to make the most of the content as its uses broaden and expand into heretofore unknown regions of science and nature." (Coxford et al. 1991, p. 4). Numerous geometries have been created that allow a variety of perspectives: finite, transformation and non-Euclidean. The mathematics used today requires students to see the interconnectedness and interdependency of these various geometries.

Cabri Geometry(239)	Markowitz (210)
Coxford (26)	Posamentier (111)
Geometer's Sketchpad (240)	Ryan (118)
Holden (189)	Thomas (147)

www.geom.umn.edu	
www.tessellations.com	

(Record your favorite Web sites here.)

Transformational Geometry

A transformation is another name for a function. Rotations around a point, translations, reflections on a line, and glide reflections are examples of transformations that are often called *rigid motions.* Noncongruent similar figures are examples of nonrigid transformations called dilations. Circular inversions include all the special transformations. The use of matrices in considering transformations serves to integrate algebra and geometry.

- What properties of plane figures are invariant under each transformation?
- What transformations are applied in physics?
- Can circular inversion be applied when some conic other than a circle is used?
- What is meant by the statement, "A set of transformations is called a group"?
- How are matrices helpful in work with transformations?
- Are poles and polars used in a type of transformation?

Brieske (170)   Smart (132)
Geometer's Sketchpad (240)   TesselMania! (242)
Moise (92)

www.ece.ucdavis.edu/~hardaker/escher	

(Record your favorite Web sites here.)

Finite Geometries

One of the most famous examples of a system of mathematical logic is Euclidean geometry. However, many simpler systems display the interrelationship of the existence of several parts that are stated in the axioms of the system without the many complications of Euclidean geometry. Such geometries are often referred to as *finite* or *miniature geometries.* Since a finite geometry requires fewer postulates than Euclidean geometry, the finite geometry provides a simpler example of a logical structure. In a finite system, it is usually easier to make a study of the consistency, completeness, and independence of a particular set of postulates.

- What is the advantage of duality in a finite metric system?
- Are there parallel lines in any of the finite geometries?
- How does one test a set of postulates for consistency, completeness, and independence?
- Does a geometry of number triples exist?

McClintock (204)   Salisbury (224)
Morgan (213)   Smart (132)

(Record your favorite Web sites here.)

Circles, Lines, Points, and Triangles in Modern Geometry

Some of the so-called modern geometries require backgrounds only in high school algebra and plane geometry. The geometry of the circle and the triangle, developed during the nineteenth century, has many special associated lines and points. A display of some of the surprising properties of these unique lines and points would be quite interesting. The exhibit should include the proof of the construction and any special applications or items of interest connected with the figure. Some of the names associated with the special points are Brianchon, Brocard, Ceva, Gergonne, Lemoine, Miquel, Nagel, Steiner, and Tarry. Additional terms associated with circles, lines, and triangles are Euler's line, the nine-point circle, Pascal's line, the pedal triangle, Simson's line, Speiker's circle, and Tucker's circle.

- What theorems in plane geometry are easily proved using Ceva's theorem or Menelaus's theorem?
- What are the trigonometric forms of these theorems?
- Can a physical interpretation be made of any of the special points or lines?
- How is the nine-point circle constructed using geometry visualization software?
- Investigate the circles of Apollonius.

Geometric superSupposer (241)
Naraine (214)   Smart (132)
Posamentier (113)   Shilgalis (227)
Salisbury (224)

(Record your favorite Web sites here.)

Non-Euclidean Geometry

The term *non-Euclidean* is used to describe systems of geometry that differ from Euclid's by at least one postulate, often the parallel postulate. Many attempts were made to prove Euclid's parallel postulate with the aid of the other postulates and axioms, but eventually the parallel postulate was proven to be independent. Elliptic and hyperbolic geometries developed from these investigations during the nineteenth century.

Taxicab geometry is a simple, non-Euclidean geometry in which the side-angle-side congruence statement for triangles does not hold. This geometry uses the coordinate plane and builds on the basic ideas of Euclidean geometry. Taxicab geometry has many practical applications and provides an excellent medium for individual exploration and creativity.

- What theorems of Euclidean geometry hold in non-Euclidean geometry?
- Is a straight line always the shortest distance between two points?
- What is the relationship between a catenary and a tractrix?
- How are non-Euclidean geometries useful in explaining temperature changes in the universe, the theory of relativity, optics, atomic physics, or the general theory of wave proportion?
- What do models of elliptic and hyperbolic geometries look like?

- Is trigonometry associated with models of elliptic and hyperbolic geometries?

Courant (24)   Millman (212)
Johnson(192)   Provost (220)
Krause (81)   Ryan (118)

mcs.open.ac.uk/tc12/nonE/nonE.html	

(Record your favorite Web sites here.)

Four-Dimensional Geometry

We live in a three-dimensional world, but can you visualize a fourth dimension? This task would be similar to someone living in two dimensions trying to visualize a three-dimensional world, a concept addressed in *Flatland,* a book by Edwin A. Abbott. The idea of a fourth dimension has been developed since 1847 and can be approached from three perspectives: choosing a fundamental element, analytic geometry, and synthetic geometry.

- What is the history of the nineteenth-century development of the concept of four dimensions?
- What use did Einstein make of the concept in the early part of the twentieth century?
- How can algebra be used to represent four or more dimensions?
- What are some differences between the geometry of three dimensions and that of four dimensions?
- What is a hypercube? A tesseract?
- What are some applications that use the concept of the fourth dimension?

Abbott (1)   Henderson (59)
Banchoff (8)   Hess (187)
Courant (24)

(Record your favorite Web sites here.)

Topology, Knots, and Surfaces

Topology is a study of properties that are not altered by continuous movement. It is an area of mathematics in which triangles and circles are considered equivalent, where a surface can have exactly one side and a donut is equivalent to a coffee cup. Euclidean geometry is just a special topic area within topology.

- What connection exists between the famous Königsberg Bridge problem, the four-color problem, the Möbius strip, and Klein's bottle?
- What happens to a Möbius strip if it is cut down the middle?
- Will the results be the same if some other method of cutting the Möbius band (e.g., cutting one-third of the way in from an edge) is tried?
- What are some tricks and puzzles based on topology?
- How is topology related to analysis?

Armstrong (6)	Newman (100)
Barnes (165)	Poggi (218)
Farmer (38)	Prasolov (114)
Jacobs (71)	

www.cs.uidaho.edu/~casey931/new_knot/index.html

(Record your favorite Web sites here.)

Modular Systems

Some frequently used systems violate many of the rules of familiar mathematics topics. Some of these are calendar numbers, clock arithmetic, finite arithmetic, and modular arithmetic. A modular system is a simplified example of a finite system that can be isolated and carefully studied. Such systems can be extended as far as interest and time permit.

- What laws hold in modular systems that do not hold in the real-number systems?
- If it is assumed that the usual definition for square root is used, do all numbers in a modulo 6 system have a single square root? Can this be generalized to other modular systems?
- Does the degree of the equation in modular arithmetic give a clue to the number of solutions expected?
- Does modular arithmetic have an application in trigonometry?
- Is there a theoretical counterpart in number congruences to the ordinary arithmetic logarithm?
- How can modulo 9 be used to test whether a natural number is a perfect square?

(Record your favorite Web sites here.)

Inequalities

In nature and in human society inequalities are the rule and equalities are the exception. Such problems as load-carrying capacity, the serviceable life of a product, and sales volume involve applications of inequalities. Inequalities are also of importance in recent developments such as game theory and linear programming.

- How are inequalities used in the Dedekind-cut concept of irrational numbers?
- What are the restrictions on the important inequality $(1 + p)^n \geq np$?
- What restriction or modification must be made in order to talk about the inequality of complex numbers?
- How are problems about maxima and minima applications of inequalities?
- How are inequalities used in modern mathematical economics, game theory, and linear programming?

(Record your favorite Web sites here.)

i, e, π, and √2̄

Irrational numbers such as e, π, and $\sqrt{2}$ are numbers that cannot be expressed as common fractions. Irrational numbers are either algebraic numbers or transcendental numbers. Algebraic numbers are roots of algebraic equations (e.g., $x^2 - 2 = 0$, where $x = \pm\sqrt{2}$). Transcendental numbers are not the roots of any algebraic equation. e and π are examples of irrational numbers that are transcendental. e is the limit value of the expression,

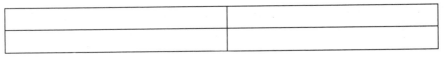

$\left(1 + \dfrac{1}{n}\right)^n$ when n increases without end.

$$e = \lim_{n \to \infty}\left(1 + \frac{1}{n}\right)^{n} = 2.718\,281\,828\,459\,045....$$

- Can a square be constructed with an area equal to that of a given circle?
- What mathematical methods can be used to compute e and π?
- What is i (as used in mathematics)?
- What formula expresses a relationship between e, i, and π?
- Can $\sqrt{2}$ be represented by a repeating decimal?

| Beckman (9) | Brueningsen (15) |
| Gullberg (55) | Wells (153) |

(Record your favorite Web sites here.)

Time Curves

The cycloid is a path traced by a fixed point on the circumference of a wheel as it rolls, without slipping, on a fixed straight line; and it has many interesting properties. It is at once the path down which a particle will fall from one given point to another in the shortest time and the path down which a particle will fall in equal time no matter what the starting point may be. The semicubical parabola is another curve associated with time. It is a curve such that in any two equal intervals of time, a particle falls equal vertical distances.

- What are the properties of other curves closely allied to the cycloid?
- Which one of the time curves has been considered a very important discovery for clock makers?
- With what other phenomenon in physics did John Bernoulli associate the brachistochrone problem in order to solve the problem?
- What other time curves are there?

    Courant (24)
    Johnson (194)
    Gullberg (55)

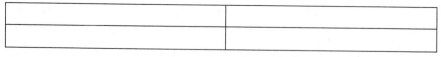

(Record your favorite Web sites here.)

Numerical Analysis

Numerical analysis is a branch of mathematics in which computational algorithms are used to find numerical solutions to problems. Engineers and scientists sometimes create equations that model physical situations but are difficult or impossible to solve by hand. The computer and modern graphing calculators are the primary tools used to implement numerical algorithms.

- What algorithms are used by the computer to find roots of polynomials or solutions to any equation?
- Why is the concept of convergence of a sequence important?
- How can someone assess the accuracy of an approximate solution when the exact answer is not known?
- Do the methods for solving systems of linear equations work for non-linear systems?
- What is a fixed point? How is that concept used in iterative algorithms?

Dugdale (179)	Nakamura (93)
Faires (36)	Phillips (108)
Kincaid (76)	

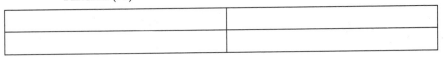

(Record your favorite Web sites here.)

Logic and Proof

Some mathematicians define proof as a valid argument based on a system of logic that convinces one's peers. To get to the point where proof is needed, we must have a conjecture to work with and a set of rules on how to proceed. In all areas of mathematics, definitions, postulates, and theorems provide the foundation for new ideas as conjectures. Before these conjectures can be accepted as theorems, they must be proved by showing they were derived from previously accepted postulates and theorems.

- What are some examples of invalid reasoning that are persuasive in politics?
- What is a tautology?
- What are some examples of paradoxes?
- What are various types of direct and indirect proof?
- What attempts have been made to use the computer to prove or disprove conjectures?

Agostini (2)   McGehee (206)
Esty (35)   Naraine (214)
Fletcher (43)   Solow (136)
Horak (190)

(Record your favorite Web sites here.)

Probability and Statistics

Mathematicians refer to probability as the systematic study of uncertainty and chance. Statistics involves collecting, organizing, describing, displaying, and interpreting data. Statistics includes making decisions and predictions on the basis of the information which has been collected or predicted. Using these skills effectively is very important in today's society, which depends heavily on technology and communication. Research scientists and mathematicians often must use statistical procedures and probability models in their experimentations.

Graphs, data, and predictions are encountered when one reads current periodicals and newspapers. Industry and government agencies formulate budgets, quotas, and general policy on the basis of theorems from probability and statistics. Some statisticians describe the evolving field of statistics as more of an art than a science.

- What does the law of large numbers imply about rolling a fair die?
- How can the results of a presidential election be predicted when fewer than 10 percent of the votes have been counted?
- What is meant by the statement, the "results are statistically significant"?
- How does the concept of *confidence interval* directly relate probability and statistics?
- Can data provided by simulating a real-world problem assist in solving the problem?

Burrill (18)   Lovitt (88)   Rector (222)
Cuff (175)   Newman (99)   Rossman (117)
Frantz (182)   MCTM/SIMMS (90)   Scheaffer (129)
Landwehr (83)   Perry (217)   Weaver (152)

(Record your favorite Web sites here.)

Mathematical Modeling

Just as a designer might construct a model of a building and then tinker with the components to see what relationships are affected by changing certain variables and what outcomes are pleasing and functional, a mathematician can construct an algebraic model to represent a situation. By choosing appropriate variables to see how relationships are affected, mathematicians can predict outcomes. Linear relationships, inverse relationships, and exponential relationships can all be used to model real-life applications. Computers and calculators may have symbolic manipulators (e.g., Mathematica or Derive) that can be used to construct mathematical models where students can manipulate data and test conjectures.

- If you throw a ball, what type of a mathematical curve results from comparing time and vertical distance during flight?
- What issues of search and control arise in artificial intelligence?
- Can a mathematical model be developed using data from pH titration of bases and acids?
- How can a computer or calculator be programmed to draw catenary curves when given the variable values?
- Can you develop a mathematical model that demonstrates queuing theory?
- Can you write a computer program that plays a game such as ticktacktoe?

Bezuszka (12)	McKim (91)
Bradie (169)	MCTM/SIMMS (90)
Casey (173)	Nord (215)
Fitzgerald (42)	Straffin (145)
Lovinelli (203)	Swetz (146)

gauss.hawcc.hawaii.edu/maths/bridge.html	
tango.mth.umassd.edu	

(Record your favorite Web sites here.)

Fractals/Chaos

Fractals can be any picture that contains self-similar images within itself. More specifically, a fractal is a rough or fragmented geometric shape that can be subdivided in parts, each of which is (at least approximately) a smaller copy of the whole. We are constantly surrounded by fractals and most people don't realize it. Computer-generated images can be fractals, but they are not the only fractals. Most occur naturally. Computer-generated fractals are created using fractal geometry.

This new kind of geometry dismisses the Euclidean way of looking at the world. A mathematician would tell you that fractals are created at the boundary between chaos and order. To understand fractals fully, one must understand chaos theory. Benoit Mandelbrot was largely responsible for the present interest in fractal geometry. He showed how fractals can occur both in mathematics and in nature.

- What ideas arise from investigating the idea of a parameter space—a map of fractals?
- What are Cauchy sequences?
- What conclusions can be drawn while investigating Möbius transformations on the Riemann sphere.
- What are Julia sets?
- Can you find several algorithms for computing fractals from iterated function systems?

Devaney (32)	Peitgen (105)
Dugdale (179)	Simmt (229)
Durkin (180)	Wahl (151)

www-groups.dcs.st-and.ac.uk/~history/Mathematicians/Mandelbrot.html	
scrtec.org/tracks/t00243.html	spanky.triumf.ca

(Record your favorite Web sites here.)

Rate of Change

Rate of change is not only represented by speed, as shown by the following example. Suppose we were to keep track of the number of people who have heard a rumor that has been started. Each day the number of people who have heard the rumor increases. We could describe the increase geometrically by plotting the points corresponding to t (number of days) and $N(t)$, the number who heard the rumor.

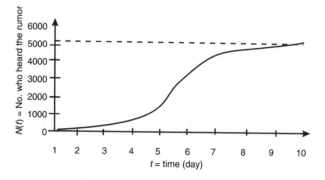

In the example above, there is a correlation between the rate at which $N(t)$ is changing and the steepness of the graph. This example illustrates one of the fundamental ideas of calculus—measuring rates of change in terms of steepness of graphs. The *derivative*, a mathematical tool to measure the rate of change, provides a numerical measure of the steepness of a curve at a particular point.

- How do rates of change relate to velocity, acceleration, and speed?
- What is the difference between speed and velocity?
- How does acceleration (rate of change of velocity) due to gravity ten miles above Earth's surface compare to what it is on Earth?
- What is the escape velocity for an object in space (i.e., the velocity at which Earth's gravity will not be able to hold the object in orbit)?
- Does an object during circular motion have a constant velocity?
- What function equals its own rate of change?

Bradie (169)	Hughes-Hallett (67)
Demana (30)	Larson (85)
Finney (41)	Nord (215)
Hopper (64)	

tango.mth.umassd.edu	

(Record your favorite Web sites here.)

Mathematics in Sports

Sporting events often provide data that can be used in students' projects. Sports medicine magazines are good sources for ideas. Comparing school records in sports can lead to projects using statistics.

- "The wave" is often seen at sporting events. How fast does it travel around a football stadium? Compare "waves" at various events.
- Compare the rate of change of your high school's track records over the past 20 years with the Olympic records during the same time period.
- Do football linemen or backs lose the most weight during a game?
- Can you compare the maximum speed of the ball in tennis, baseball, badminton, and table tennis?
- How long can a basketball player "hang" in the air? Why?

> May (209)
> Sadovskiĭ (120)
> Townsend (148)

(Record your favorite Web sites here.)

Combinatorics

Combinatorics is a branch of mathematics that is concerned with the selection of objects, usually called members or elements of a set. Historically, it was often used to perform magic tricks with numbers. Combinatorical mathematics determines odds or likelihood in games of chance. Today, combinatorics is widely applied in many areas of mathematics that involve probability and statistics.

- How many ways can the football coach select a team of 11 players if he has 37 players on the team?
- Can the number combinations be determined by using Pascal's Triangle?
- How many ways can the order vary if you decide to visit 3 states in the continental U.S.? 10 states? All 50 states?
- What are Latin squares, and how are they related to statistical analysis?
- Research the mathematics of lotteries.

  Brualdi (14)
  Jackson (70)

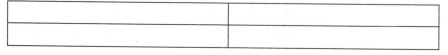

(Record your favorite Web sites here.)

Applied Analysis

Applied analysis procedures include such topics as equations, functions, matrix algebra, linear programming, multivariate analysis, and complex applications using probability and statistics. Applications cover such diverse areas as mathematics of finance, biology, medicine, sociology, psychology, ecology, statistics, earth science, and archaeology.

- Can you find a geometric solution of a system of inequalities by using linear programming?
- How is input-output analysis used to analyze the production of industrial sectors of an economy?
- How is linear programming used to maximize and minimize a function that is subject to certain restrictions?

- How does the simplex method solve a standard linear programming problem?
- What is the rule of 78, and how is it applied to paying off a loan before the last payment is due?

Haeussler (57)	Stewart (143)
Hoffman (188)	Straffin (145)
Hughes-Hallett (68)	

(Record your favorite Web sites here.)

Linear Algebra

Linear algebra involves the concepts of vectors, matrices, mappings and determinants, and their relationships to each other. Linear programming, systems of linear equations, vector spaces and subspaces, affine lines and Euclidean spaces, and mappings are all elements of linear algebra. These topics provide a variety of problem-solving tools in many areas. For example, urban planners are interested in maximizing their ability to remove waste matter subject to restrictions on the equipment and labor force available. Airlines wish to maximize flight time per airplane subject to pilot availability, maintenance restrictions, passenger numbers, and other factors.

- What is the duality theorem?
- How is the fundamental pivot-exchange algorithm used to solve problems that minimize travel to a number of towns connected by several possible routes?
- What is a matrix? Why is it useful in mathematics?
- Can you solve an application problem by using mappings?
- What is a determinant? Why are determinants useful when solving systems of equations?

Datta (29)
Hoenig (63)
Wicks (156)

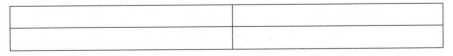

(Record your favorite Web sites here.)

Abstract Algebra

Sets, functions, and equivalence relations, as with many other branches of mathematics, are part of the foundations of algebra. Abstract algebra includes numerous other topics such as rings, groups, and field theory.

- What is the fundamental theorem of algebra?
- What is a complex number, and what are the field properties of the complex numbers?
- What is the difference between a ring and a field?
- Develop a field with a finite set of elements.
- Is it possible for a proper subgroup of a nonabeliean group to be abelian?
- In modular arithmetic what are residue classes? Do all elements in a modular arithmetic system have additive inverses? Multiplicative inverses?

Anderson (5)	Johnson (193)
Fletcher (43)	NCTM (95)
Goodwan (52)	

(Record your favorite Web sites here.)

3

Looking for Specific Ideas

THERE is no one source of ideas for projects; an idea can come in various ways and from many sources. Conferences and conversations with teachers, mathematicians, scientists, other students, community members, and online mentors are sources of suggestions. Ideas can also be obtained from listings of previous mathematics projects, from reports of fair winners in talent searches, from articles in magazines, and from newspaper stories concerning mathematics. Mathematics and science books and periodicals are fertile sources of ideas for projects. An idea can begin with a statement in an article, a question, or a reference that causes the student to wonder why or why not and motivates the student to investigate the problem further. Internet WWW sites also provide up-to-date and extensive information. For example, to explore potential *Mathematics Teacher* or *Mathematics Teaching in the Middle School* references, go to the NCTM Web site. For instructions, see Appendix E.

www.nctm.org	

(Record your favorite Web sites here.)

LEADING QUESTIONS

One way for a teacher to generate topics for projects is to pose leading questions like the ones below, to which the answers are known. These questions may stimulate students' curiosity and lead them to further study in theoretical and applied mathematics.

1. Can you describe an experiment that uses a dependent variable and an independent variable?
2. Can a set contain itself as an element?
3. Why are there only five Platonic solids?
4. What is a best-fit line for a given set of data?
5. Which are more numerous, the points of a line segment or the points of a line?
6. How does a pendulum's length affect its periodicity?

7. What are some applications of symmetry in nature?

8. What is meant by the statement, "The average height of boys today is five centimeters more than that of boys a generation ago"?

9. What are some applications of mathematics to nature?

10. Can a segment of length $\sqrt{2}$ be constructed using a straightedge and compass only?

11. What is the triangle of smallest perimeter that can be inscribed in a given triangle?

12. How many mail routes must the post office maintain in order to serve all parts of a city without having more than one route in any section?

IDEAS FOR REPORTS AND THINGS TO CONSTRUCT

Many students may not have the desire or the time to do a long-term project involving experimentation like those discussed earlier. They might, however, find it interesting to do a report, either oral or written, on a mathematician, scientist, or statistician. A student may also be interested in researching and reporting on a number theory topic. Such reports can be a part of classwork and might encourage more students' interest in various aspects of mathematics. Applications and constructions provide other challenges.

Gullberg (55)

forum.swarthmore.edu	

(Record your favorite Web sites here.)

Mathematicians

The lives of famous mathematicians, both men and women, are very interesting and can prompt informative documentation reports. Women have made significant contributions to the development of mathematics from ancient times. Historically, however, little attention was given to their work. A noticeable change in society's recognition of, and appreciation for, women's contributions to mathematics has occurred only within the last three or four decades. See Appendix B for a list of mathematicians by subject area.

Cooney (22)
Grinstein (54)
Stein (142)

(Record your favorite Web sites here.)

Some of the people who made outstanding contributions to mathematics before the twentieth century are Abel, Agnesi, Archimedes, Cantor, Desargues, Descartes, duChatelet, Eratosthenes, Euler, Fermat, Galois, Gauss, Germain, Herschel, Hypatia, Kovalevsky, Leibniz, Lobachevski, Lovelace, Newton, Pythagoras, Riemann, Saccheri, Somerville, and Thales.

Modern mathematicians include Birkhoff, Blackwell, Chern, Conway, Coxeter, Diaconis, Erdos, Gardner, Graham, Granville, Halmos, Hilton, Kemeny, Kline, Knuth, Mandelbrot, Noether, Pollak, Polya, Ramanujan, Rees, Reid, Rudin, Robbins, Smullyan, Taussky-Todd, Tucker, Ulam, Whitehead, and Young.

Albers (3, 4)	Grinstein (54)
Bennett (166)	Knauff (80)
Cooney (22)	Pappas (103)
Fauvel (39)	Spencer (139)

www.scottlan.edu/lriddle/women/women.html
www-groups.dcs.st-and.ac.uk:80/~history/index.html
aleph0.clarku.edu/~djoyce/mathhist/mathhist.html
aleph0.clarku.edu/~djoyce/hilbert/problems.html

(Record your favorite Web sites here.)

Statisticians

Statistics, one of the fastest growing branches of the mathematical sciences, is a relative newcomer to the grades K–12 school curriculum. The ideas of probability and statistics come from the earliest mathematicians. Students might enjoy reading about statisticians such as Bernoulli, Cardano, DeMoivre, Fermat, Galileo, Huygens, Pepys, and Wallis. Some twentieth-century statisticians are Bailar, Box, Cochran, Cox, Deming, R. A. Fisher, Hunter, Martin, Mosteller, Norwood, Scheffe, Snedecor, and Tukey.

Weaver (152)

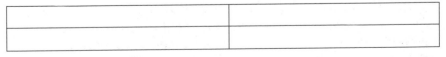

(Record your favorite Web sites here.)

Scientists

A number of people have made exceptional contributions to mathematics even though their main interest areas were outside mathematics. Some of these are Buffon, Bolzano, Durer, Napier, and Pascal.

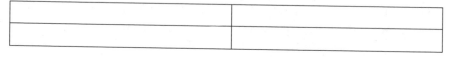

(Record your favorite Web sites here.)

Number Theory

Students will find that the history, relationships, and occurrences of certain constants are very interesting. Some of the more common constants are $0, 1, i, e, \pi$, and ϕ. The first five of these constants all occur in the equation $e^{i\pi} + 1 = 0$, where $i = \sqrt{-1}$.

The history of the introduction of 0 is interesting and enlightening. Approximating the value of π and e can be done in various ways. Buffon devised a way of approximating π by probability methods. The value of π can be approximated by tossing a coin or a needle. The value of e can be approximated by spinning a needle or by randomly drawing numbers or marbles from a bag. The mathematical theory behind these methods is rather interesting. The symbol ϕ, associated with the golden section, occurs not only in mathematics but also with phenomena in nature.

Andreasen (162)	Long (87)
Green (53)	Seymour (126)
Lauber (201)	Spencer (137)
Lemon (202)	vosSavant (150)

www.geom.umn.edu/apps/gallery.html	

(Record your favorite Web sites here.)

Geometric Constructions

Constructions of geometric figures are interesting and motivating to many students. Straightedge-and-compass constructions are easy to do and produce very pleasing designs. If a greater challenge is needed, restrictions can be placed on the type of tools used or the method of using them. Some of the easiest constructions are regular polygons, triangles, and circles that contain hexagonal figures. Use of drawing utilities on computers and graphing calculators can enhance the ability of students to deduce more properties. More complex curves include cardioids, catenaries, cissoids, conchoids, and cycloids. The problem of Apollonius, which involves circles, will appeal to some students.

Numerous points and lines encountered in the study of geometry are of interest. These include Euler lines, Simson lines, Brocard points, and Gergonne points. Some of these can be studied in connection with the nine-point circle. The construction of three-dimensional models of polyhedra can be fascinating.

Cabri Geometry (239)	Posamentier (111)
Courant (24)	Seymour (125)
Geometer's Sketchpad (240)	Smart (132)
Hilton (61)	Thomas (147)
Lyng (89)	Wenninger (154)

(Record your favorite Web sites here.)

Applications

Many aspects of mathematics have applications in such areas as art, music, nature, photography, and building structures. Other applications deal with how mathematics is used in a particular occupation or how it has affected physical theories, political thought, social science, or ancient cultures. Since these topics are so diverse, students should read books, newspapers, and magazines and access the Internet as excellent sources of current information.

Austin (7)	MCTM/SIMMS (90)
Bezuszka (12)	NCTM(94)
Garland (48)	Sadovskií (120)
Haak(186)	Sagan (121)
Houston (66)	Straffin (145)

gauss.hawcc.hawaii.edu/maths/bridge.html	

(Record your favorite Web sites here.)

TITLES OF PROJECTS

The following organized list of project titles, all of which have been entered in a science fair or in a science talent search, can be used by teachers as a beginning point for classroom discussions of possible topics. Students can use the list to give them some direction in their search for potential projects. Titles have been divided into broad topic areas and also grouped by possible grade level.

Grades 6–8

Algebra, Game Theory, and Theory of Numbers
- Number Systems
- A Comparison of the Septimal and Decimal Systems
- Proof of Some Properties of Fibonacci Numbers
- The Pythagorean Triples
- Elementary Number Generators
- The History of Pi

Analysis
- Arranging Fractions between 0 and 1 in Ascending Order of Numerical Value

Arithmetic
- From Sticks to Numerals
- Roman Numerals and the Abacus
- The World's Oldest Adding Machine and How It Works
- Napier's Rods
- The Algorithm of Euclid
- Mathematics to Base n ($n \neq 10$)
- Comparison of Number Systems
- Extensions of Arithmetic Operations
- The Duodecimal System
- An Arithmetical Method to Find the Nth Root of a Number
- A Number System to an Irrational Base
- Investigations in the Theory of Decimal Expansions

Computers, Logic, and Numeral Analysis
- Ciphers, Codes, and the Way They Are Broken
- Calculating Machines of the Future
- Stonehenge—a Neolithical Calculator
- Number Systems and Computers
- The Abacus versus the Calculator

Geometry, Topology

- Which Figure Has the Greatest Area?
- Finding the Area of an Ellipse
- The Great Icosahedron
- Geometric Mobile
- Geometry by Paper Folding
- From Squares to Circles
- Euclidean Constructions with Arbitrary-Sized Instruments
- Geometric Constructions with Tools other than Compass and Straightedge
- Folding Polyhedrons
- Pascal's Pyramid
- Nine Postulates for Euclidean Geometry
- Primitive Geometry Taken from the Indians
- Geometry of Bubbles and Liquid Film
- How Eratosthenes Measured the Circumference of the Earth
- Geometric Dissections—Tangrams
- A Discussion of the Four-Color Problem
- What Is Topology?

Statistics and Probability

- How to Lie with Statistics
- Mathematical Probability and Mendel's Law
- Polynomials of Best Fit by the Method of Least Squares

Miscellaneous

- The Magic of Mathematics
- Mosaics: Math Invades Art
- Optical Illusions
- Indirect Measurement
- History of the Calendar
- Symmetry in Nature
- A Fourth Dimension
- Roots by Rates
- Proof by Nines
- Finding Inaccessible Distance

Grades 9–12

Algebra, Game Theory, and Theory of Numbers

- Algebra of Sets
- New Relations for Fibonacci-Like Series
- Properties of Fibonacci-Like Sequences
- Development of Class-Two Perfect Numbers
- Consecutive Prime Powers
- Unitary Superperfect Numbers
- An Investigation of the Twin Primes Problem
- Natural Logarithms of Complex Numbers
- Convergence of Continued Fractions
- Special Matrix Exponential Forms
- Densities of Nondeficient Numbers in Several Integer Sequences
- Pascal's Triangle in Three Dimensions
- Demonstration of the Inadequacy of Induction in Mathematical Proofs
- The Commutative Ring and the Set of Multiplicative Structures in an Additive Abelian Group
- The Use of Game Theory to Determine Courses of Action
- An Investigation of Pythagorean N-tuples and Similar Diophantine Equations
- Rotation Groups
- General Solution of a Linear Diophantine Equation of Three Variables
- Matrix Inversion by Means of the Cayley-Hamilton Theorem
- The Number of Ways to Represent the Reciprocal of an Integer as the Sum of the Reciprocal of Two Integers
- Factorable Sets of Integers of the Form $ak + b$
- Matrix Representation of the Chromosome Theory
- Electronic Graphical Representation of Any Second-Degree Equation
- Experimental Treatment of Square Root as Infinite Geometric Progressions
- Hypercomplex Numbers
- Linkages and the Application of Their Properties to Solving Equations
- Group Theory of the Equilateral Triangle
- Constructing a Mathematical Ring
- Proof of a Mathematical Theory in the Generation of Langford's Numbers

- The Function $x^y = y^x$
- A Study of Fermat's Equation
- A Topic in Diophantine Analysis: Cole Numbers
- A New Graphic Study of Magic Squares of the Fourth Order
- Pauli Matrices as an Example of a Group
- Bicomplex Numbers
- Multiplication Table for a Noncommutative Group
- Algebraic Solution to Electrical Circuits
- Finite Sums of Polynomials
- A New Sieve for Finding Prime Number
- The Analysis of Algebraic Congruences in One Unknown
- Investigation of Odd Perfect Numbers
- On the Number of Nth Roots in Finite Abelian Groups
- Symmetric Functions of Roots
- The Analysis of Symmetric Groups of Degree Four and Their Relation to Eigen Values
- The Graphical Representation of Complex Roots of Quadratic and Cubic Equations
- The Flip Side of Fibonacci
- Mathematics and Switching Circuits
- The "Proof" of Goldbach's Conjecture by Means of Probability
- Symmetry in Equations
- An Algebraic Approach to the Fourth Dimension
- An Investigation of Moduli Systems and Pascal's Triangle
- An Investigation of Perfect Numbers Both Even and Odd
- Inequalities Related to Fibonacci Numbers
- A Fifth-Dimension Analog of a Binomial Cube
- The Development of a General Semigroup

Analysis
- Transfinite Mathematics
- Convex Smooth Curves
- A Nondifferentiable Function
- Minimal Surface Area Experiments with Soap Films
- Hyperbolic Functions and Related Infinite Series in the Complex Domain

- A Development of a Power Series for the Sum of the Rth Term of the First N Numbers
- The Application of Calculus to the Solution of Game Matrices
- A New Method of Summing Certain Infinite Series
- Elliptic Integrals
- The Brachistochrone-Tautochrone Problem
- The Development of a Term-Difference Method for Function of Finite Sets
- $F(x) = F(1 - x)$ and Other Mathematical Investigations
- The Evaluation of Real Integrals by Means of Complex Residues
- The Diagonal Sums of General Slope in a Right Pascal Triangle and Their Relation to Fibonacci-Type Sequences
- Ordering the Set of Complex Numbers
- The Calculus of Finite and Infinitesimal Ratios
- The Concept of Number Applied to Infinite Sets
- The Application of Cybernetics to the Solution of Differential Equations
- N-Point Tensor Calculus
- The Curvature-of-Droplets Comparison of Set Theory with Elements and Compounds
- A Discussion of Large Numbers with Special Application to Infinities of Varying Size
- A Logical Analysis of Infinity and Infinite Set Theory

Computers, Logic, and Numerical Analysis
- Set Theory with Application to Symbolic Logic
- Empirical Variation on Newton's Method
- The Derivation of Rules for Programming the Game of Ticktacktoe
- Symbolic Compiler for Arithmetic and Logical Programs
- The Digital Classification of Words for Decoding
- The Braille-Scuber—an Original Use of a Digital Computer
- An Approximation to Euler's Constant by Probability Theory and Random Numbers Applied to High-Speed Electronic Computers
- A Decimal-to-Binary Converter and Binary Adder
- An Electronic Analog Computer for the Solution of Cubic Equations by Cardano's Formula
- Ciphers, Codes, and the Way They Are Broken

- A Binary Relay Computer and Simple Transistor Circuits
- The Design, Development, and Construction of a Small Binary Digital Computer
- Electronic Nim Partner
- Digital Quadratics Computer
- The Semiautomatic Binary Digital Computer
- An Analog Computer to Solve Combined Charles's and Boyle's Laws
- The Formation of Digital Root Series
- Cybernetic Computers
- An Electrical Computer Capable of Proving Thousands of Geometric Theorems
- An Application of a Digital Computer to the Solution of Rectangular Games
- Elementary Random Number Generators

Geometry
- Finite Projective Geometry and Abelian Groups
- Quasi-Brocard Geometry
- Algorithmic Methods for Generating Reverse Theorems
- Locus by Light
- Plane Projections of the Earth
- The Hyperbolic Paraboloid
- Biangular Systems of Coordinates
- The Superbola $Y = X^x$
- Mascheroni's Constructions
- The Finite Solid Geometry System
- Duality in Points and Lines
- Locus in Space
- The Geometry of a Catenary
- Bipolar Geometry
- The Triangle Theorem of Desargues
- Investigations into Areas of Fractal Patterns
- Pass Filtering on Fractal Dimension
- The Fractal Nature of a Chaotic Attractor
- Viscous Fingers as Fractals
- A Continuous Conic Section Generator

- The Hyperboloid
- Euclidean Constructions with Arbitrary-Sized Instruments
- Place Intersections in N Dimensions
- Pascal's Pyramid
- Conic Sections and Allied Surfaces
- Investigating the Nine-Point Circle in Three-Space
- An Extension of the Theorem of Pythagoras
- A Geometry of the Triangle of Progressions
- Nine Postulates for Euclidean Geometry
- Primitive Geometry Taken from the Indians
- Limitations on Euclidean Geometry
- The Geometry of Bubbles and Liquid Film
- Chameleonic Cubes
- The Integral Right Triangle
- Theory of Rotations of Coordinate Axes in N-Space
- Angular Coordinates
- Graphs of Conic Sections for Complex Values of the Variable
- Solving the 60° and 120° Triangle
- The Mathematics of Crystals
- Quadric Surfaces
- A Comparison of Three Geometric Transformations
- How Eratosthenes Measured the Circumference of the Earth
- Euclid's and Lobachevski's Assumptions on Parallels
- A Determinate Formula for the Area of the Two-Dimensional Polygonal Figures
- The Analytic Geometry of Oblique Coordinates with Special Attention to the Plotting of Inequality Relationships
- Finding the Equation for the Inversions of a Curve Centered at the Origin
- The Geometric Foundations of the Theory of Relativity
- Analytic Geometry in N Dimensions
- A Mathematical Analysis of the Locus of Points on a Rotating Reuleaux Polygon
- An Investigation of the Trochoid Family of Curves
- Cylindrical Projections and Their Applications

- Conjugate Coordinates in the Study of the Cardioid
- The Determination of Equations of Complex Curves' Surfaces in Space
- Aristotelian Space—a Research into the Logical-Prospective Properties of Pascal's Table
- Brocard Points in Aviation
- The Centroids of Plane Figures
- Gergonne's Problem
- Projected Geometric Progression
- An Extension of the Classical Problem of Apollonius into Three Dimensions
- The First Twelve-Point Sphere of an Orthogonal Tetrahedron
- Vector Applications to Ratios in Triangles
- An Investigation of Periodic Linear Fractional Transformation
- Developing Three-Dimensional Space-Time Geometry
- The Multidimensional Evolution of Certain Polygons
- An Extension of Euler's Polyhedral Formula to N Dimensions
- Furthering Pappus's Extension
- Geometry on a Cylindrical Surface
- Producing Geometric Forms with Mass
- Studying the Twist and Turn of a Third-Dimensional Curve
- Finite Coordinate Systems on the Surface of a Sphere
- Geometric (and Relativity) Concepts of Four Dimensions
- Geometry of N Dimensions with Emphasis on Topologies
- Graphing in Four Dimensions
- Fourth-Dimensional Tetra-Quadric Surfaces and Their Application
- Fourth-Dimension Space-Time Continuum
- N-Dimensional Conic Sections
- The Quartic Curves
- Shells and the Geometric Spiral
- A Proof of Cavalieri's Theorem
- Optics of the Ellipse with Emphasis on Parallel Incident Rays
- Bubble Curves and the Roulettes of Conic Sections
- Measuring the Earth and Distance to the Moon by Simple Geometry
- Pappus's Extension of the Pythagorean Theorem
- Geometric Interpretation of Super Perfect Numbers

- Geometry of Parangular Complex Inverse, and Complex Inverse Polygons
- Curves of Constant Width

Statistics and Probability

- How to Lie with Statistics
- The Number e by Spinning a Needle
- Mathematical Aspects of Population Growth
- Mathematical Probability and Mendel's Law
- A Statistical Analysis of Background Radiation in a Selected City
- A Statistical Study of Finger Length Variations in Adolescent Hands
- The Error Curve in Modern Science and Mathematics
- A Statistical Analysis of Fossil Species
- Driving Fatalities
- A Triangular Proof of the Law of Probability
- The Correlation between Mathematics and Musical Ability
- A Statistical Analysis of Temperature Variations with Distance
- Probability in Genetic Domination
- A Vector Approach to Statistics
- Mathematics and Games of Chance
- Mathematical Analysis of Batting Performance in the Game of Baseball
- Polynomials of Best Fit by the Method of Least Squares
- A Statistical Study of Auto Engine Repairs
- A Statistical Study of Some of the Factors That Influence People in Buying
- Determining π by Probability
- Geometric Figures in Probability
- The Tetrachoric Correlation

Trigonometry

- Graphing Trigonometric Functions on Rectangular and Polar Coordinates
- Trigonometric Functions from the Unit Circle
- Minkowskian Trigonometry
- Trigonometric Curves and the Unit Circle
- Generalized Trigonometric Functions and Spiral Trigonometry

Topology

- Combinatorial Topology
- One-Sided Surfaces
- A Discussion of the Four-Color Problem
- Topology, One-sided Surfaces, and the Königsberg Problem
- The Relation of Continuity between Regions of a Map Applied to the Proof of the Four-Color Problem
- A Topological Study of Paradromic Curves
- Constructing a Klein Bottle
- The Proof of Euler's Formula and Its Use in Proving the Five-Color Problem
- Variations of the Möbius Strip and Other Problems of Topology
- Topological Analysis by Means of Dual Maps
- A Solution to a Famous Eight-Color Problem and Its Generalization
- "Rubber Geometry"—Some Properties of Topological Surfaces
- The Topology of Knots

Miscellaneous

- Mosaics by Reflections
- Mathematics in Music and Sound
- Chinese Rings
- Function before Fashion—Mathematical Designs
- A Mathematical Theory of Relativity
- Mathematical Principles of Particle Acceleration
- Models and Mathematics of the Vanguard Rocket
- Analyzing Hurricane Paths
- Mathematical Models of Yeast Growth
- The Relationship between Mathematical Formulae and Marine Mollusk Shell Growth

SOME UNSOLVED PROBLEMS

It is easy for someone who has not studied mathematics deeply to conclude that mathematics is one discipline that has answers for all its problems. However, many problems are yet to be solved. Some are much older than others, but as old problems are solved, new ones arise. Previously unsolved problems have been solved by the application of new methods or

new approaches. The four-color problem remains unsolved using traditional approaches, but many mathematicians believe it has been solved using
the computer.

Guy (56)
Klee (78)

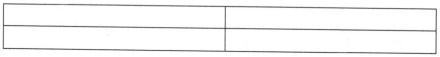

(Insert your favorite Web sites here.)

*The following list of unsolved problems might inspire some interesting pro-
jects.*

1. Goldbach conjectured that every even integer $N > 2$ is the sum of two
   primes and that every sufficiently large integer $N \geq 6$ is the sum of three
   primes. Was he right?

2. Can an odd integer be perfect? How many perfect numbers are there?

3. How many pairs of amicable numbers exist?

4. Can a simple formula be found such that when a prime number is given,
   the next larger prime number can be found?

5. Is Kepler's conjunctive true, that is, the densest possible packing of
   same-sized spheres is the triangular pyramid arrangement, which fills
   $\pi/\sqrt{18}$ (74 percent) of space?

6. Are there infinitely many twin primes?

7. How can a traveling sales representative plan an itinerary for a trip to an
   arbitrary number of cities on a map to make the trip as short as possible?

8. Is there a mathematical method to analyze the turbulence of traffic on a
   four-lane highway?

9. Can a machine be designed to duplicate precisely the human thought
   process?

10. Can a consistent mathematical meaning to the common intuitive notion
    of straightness be found?

11. Can a short proof of the four-color problem be found?

Resources

ANNOTATED BIBLIOGRAPHY OF INTERNET SITES, MATHEMATICS BOOKS, PERIODICALS, ARTICLES, AND BOOK CHAPTERS

THE Internet, mathematics books, and periodicals provide a fertile source of ideas for mathematics projects. A number of lists of mathematics books suitable for middle and high school libraries are available. A careful selection of materials from the lists given here will provide good primary and general reference sources to stimulate ideas for mathematics projects. The Internet provides new and revised web pages as a current resource accessible from most public libraries, school, or home.

An excellent source is *Students and Research: Practical Strategies for Science Classrooms and Competitions* (Couthron [25]), which was written to make it easier for classroom teachers to teach students the skills they need to successfully conduct, analyze, and report an experiment successfully.

Internet Sites
(other specific sites mentioned with project topics)

ericir.syr.edu

AskERIC is the Internet-based education information service of the Educational Resources Information Center (ERIC). AskERIC is composed of three major components: AskERIC Q & A Service (allows teachers to send a message requesting education information, with a 48 hour response time); AskERIC Virtual Library (selected resources for education and general interest including access to the ERIC Database and full-text ERIC Digests, archives of education-related listserves, and remote access to other Internet sites); the AskEric Research & Development team.

www.scri.fsu.edu/~dennisl/CMS/sf/sf.html

California Science Fair—Getting Started with Your Project provides great step-by-step guidelines for science fairs in California and other locations. Some aspects can be adapted for mathematics fairs.

```
www.enc.org
```

Eisenhower National Clearinghouse for Mathematics and Sciences Education includes many features such as ENC's Digital Dozen, which provides links to thirteen mathematics and science sites. New links are presented each month.

```
www.isd77.k12.mn.us/resources/cf/SciProjIntro.html
```

Experimental Science Projects offers an introductory-level guide with basic information for doing a science project.

```
www.geom.umn.edu
```

The Geometry Center provides links to a wide variety of geometry resources on the Internet, including interactive applications, multimedia documents, course materials, and archives.

```
naic.nasa.gov
```

Guide to NASA On-line Resources is a network resource of interest to users of the NASA Science Internet, especially information provided by different NASA Centers.

```
work.ucsd.edu:5141/cgi-bin/http_webster?
```

Hypertext Webster Gateway provides a point-and-click interface for accessing various dictionary services on Internet, including definitions of mathematics words.

```
www.cut-the-knot.com
```

Interactive Mathematics Miscellany and Puzzles offers examples of high school students' projects in many areas, including teachers' descriptions of the projects and students' guidelines. Ideas for geometry using Geometer's Sketchpad, and more.

```
ipl.org/
```

Internet Public Library provides access through the Reference Center and Materials References to engage WWW sites, including Bibliographies of Women Mathematicians, Frequently Asked Questions (FAQ) about Mathematics, Fractal FAQ, and an online mathematics dictionary.

```
sln.fi.edu/tfi/hotlists/math.html
```

Mathematics Hotlist provides point-and-click access to WWW sites for more than 70 mathematics-related topics and people.

www.c3.lanl.gov/mega-math/welcome.html

The MegaMath Project is intended to bring unusual and important mathematical ideas to elementary school classrooms so that young people and their teachers can think about them together.

www.nctm.org

National Council of Teachers of Mathematics (NCTM) site includes a listing of NCTM's educational materials and journals as well as a help line.

www.omsi.edu/educprogs/YOUNGSCHOLARS/

Oregon Museum of Science and Industry Young Scholars page

www.montana.edu/wwwsimms

SIMMS IM Project Overview gives information about the SIMMS grades 9–12 Integrated Mathematics curriculum, which includes real-world applications and research projects.

www.si.edu

The Smithsonian Institution, home page for the Smithsonian, America's treasure house for learning

www.scottlan.edu/lriddle/women/women.html

Women Mathematicians, an ongoing project of biographies of women mathematicians by students in mathematics classes at Agnes Scott College in Atlanta.

Mathematics Books

The following books listed are *primary source* books for project-related work:

Cohen, Marcus, Edward D. Gaughan, Arthur Knoebel, Douglas S. Kurtz, and David Pengelley. *Student Research Projects in Calculus.* Mathematical Association of America, 1992.

More than 100 projects are presented in single and multivariable calculus. Teacher notes contain information on prerequisites, list the main topics the project explores, and suggest helpful hints.

Couthron, Julia H., Ronald N. Giese, and Richard J. Rezba. *Students and Research: Practical Strategies for Science Classrooms and Competitions.* 2nd ed. Dubuque, Iowa: Kendall/Hunt Publishing Co., 1993.

This book was written to make it easier for classroom teachers to teach students the skills they need to conduct, analyze, and report an experiment successfully. The book has also focused attention on assessment and ways for formulating research questions.

Dalton, Leroy C., and Henry C. Snyder, eds. *Topics for Mathematics Clubs.* 2nd ed. National Council of Teachers of Mathematics, 1983.

Stimulates interest in mathematical investigation through exciting topics not usually discussed in the classroom. Encourages students' presentation of related subtopics. Bibliographies suggest further reading. Intended for students in grades 9–12.

DeMeulemeester, Katie. *Math Projects: Organization, Implementation, and Assessment.* Dale Seymour, 1995.

This book helps the grades 6–12 students navigate all phases of a mathematics project.

Gerver, Robert. *Writing Math Research Papers.* Key Curriculum Press, 1997.

This is a text for grades 10–12 students as well as a resource for teachers. The book systematically describes how to write a research paper, including prewriting and the postwriting follow-up of presentation. The book also provides a list of research topics.

Sachs, Leroy, ed. *Projects to Enrich School Mathematics,* Level 3. 2nd ed. National Council of Teachers of Mathematics, 1988.

Supplies challenging projects for secondary school students. Provides enrichment materials requiring from ten to thirty hours of independent study and writing. Includes hints, drawings, references, and ideas for further investigation as well as teacher notes, with essential information and solutions.

Seymour, Dale. *Encyclopedia of Math Topics and References. A Resource for Projects and Explorations.* Dale Seymour, 1995.

This unique resource provides 262 mathematics projects ideas at three levels of difficulty. Topics include catenary curves, hexaflexagons, odds, spirals, data analysis, mathematics and music, and consumer mathematics.

Souviney, R., M. Britt, S. Gargiulo, and P. Hughes. *Mathematical Investigations.* Dale Seymour, 1990.

Meaningful mathematical experiences with interconnected lessons and real-world activities that can extend into projects. The activities, designed for grades 8–12 gifted students, engage students in many applications of algebra, geometry, graphing, counting, probability, and statistics.

The following books are good *general resources* for projects:

Austin, Joe Dan, ed. *Applications of Secondary School Mathematics.* National Council of Teachers of Mathematics, 1991.

Seventy-eight articles selected from fifteen years of the *Mathematics Teacher.* Emphasizes the use of real-world applications in arithmetic, geometry, algebra, trigonometry, elementary analysis, calculus, probability, and statistics.

Banchoff, Thomas F. *Beyond the Third Dimension: Geometry, Computer Graphics, and Higher Dimensions.* Mathematical Association of America, 1996.

The book expands the reader's visual boundaries as he or she learns how a dimension can represent energy, temperature, and numerous other variables, including time. The reader learns how the concept of dimension plays an unexpected role in fields as diverse as medicine and modern art, and also in our everyday lives.

Billstein, Rick, and Jim Williamson. *MathThematics. Books 1, 2, & 3 (SE and TE).* McDougal Littell, 1999.

A *Standards*-based, grades 6–8 mathematics series written by the National Science Foundation Six Through Eight Mathematics (STEM) Project. Progressive mathematics presented through thematic modules is explored with appropriate projects suggested.

Burrill, Gail, M. Clifford, P. Hopfensperger, R. Scheaffer, and J. Witmer. *Data Driven Mathematics Series.* Dale Seymour, 1997–98.

Titles included are *Exploring Centers*—students explore the concept of center through a variety of activities related to topics in geometry; *Advanced Modeling and Matrices*—students are introduced to problems with several possible explanatory variables, matrices are used to express the problem in mathematical terms, and matrix operations are used as a tool in the analysis; *Exploring Symbols: An Introduction to Expressions and Functions*—a spreadsheet formulation of problems is used so symbols acquire a natural meaning as column labels; and *Exploring Projects: Planning and Conducting Surveys & Experiments*—students are led step-by-step through the processes and key components of a successful project including problem formulation; data collection, analysis, and interpretation; teamwork; and managing data.

Campbell, Douglas, and John Higgins. *Mathematics: People, Problems, Results.* Vols. 1, 2, and 3. Chapman & Hall, 1984.

Extensive collection of readings about mathematics: how it developed and philosophical and psychological implications.

Courant, Richard, Herbert Robbins, and Ian Stewart. *What Is Mathematics? An Elementary Approach to Ideas and Methods.* 2nd ed. Oxford, 1996.

Originally written for mature readers, now a classic. Excellent introductory ideas on number systems, geometric construction, number theory, topology, and postulation systems.

Fauvel, John, and Jeremy Gray. *The History of Mathematics: A Reader.* Macmillan, 1996.

Readings cover earliest times to the twentieth century, including discussion of the origins of counting to the application of electronic computers, and from Euclid's Elements to Cantor's continuum hypothesis.

Gardner, Martin. *Penrose Tiles to Trapdoor Ciphers ... and the Return of Dr. Matrix.* Mathematical Association of America, 1997.

A collection of problems, puzzles, and paradoxes from Gardner's "Mathematical Games" columns in the *Scientific American.* Topics include pool-ball triangles, Penrose tiles, Mandelbrot's fractals, negative numbers, and Conway's surreal numbers.

Garland, Trudi H., and Charity Vaughan Kahn. *Math and Music, Harmonious Connections.* Dale Seymour, 1995.

This book explores the fascinating relationship between numbers and music. Proportions, patterns, Fibonacci numbers, geometric transformations, trigonometric functions, fractals, and other mathematical concepts are inherent in music.

Gnanadesikan, Mirudulla, Richard L. Scheaffer, and Jim Swift. *The Art and Techniques of Simulation.* Dale Seymour, 1986.

Students solve practical problems using simple simulations to develop the idea of mathematical modeling (grades 7–12).

Gullberg, Jan. *Mathematics from the Birth of Numbers.* W. W. Norton, 1997.

This one-volume mathematics encyclopedia is an excellent resource for a middle school or high school mathematics department. Its easily readable format covers mathematics from its beginnings to contemporary issues.

Henry, Boyd. *Explorations in Mathematics for the Secondary Student.* Everyday Learning, 1994.

Twenty-six investigations for students to explore arithmetic, algebra, and geometry topics. Answers are included.

Hirsch, Christian R., and Robert A. Lang, eds. *Activities for Active Learning and Teaching: Selections from the "Mathematics Teacher."* National Council of Teachers of Mathematics, 1993.

A rich resource of classroom activities for grades 7–10 organized into chapters on problem solving, numeracy, algebra and graphs, geometry and visualization, and data analysis and probability. Selected activities supporting the *Standards* engage students in the use of manipulatives, calculators, graphing calculators, and computers. Each activity includes a teacher's guide with objectives, materials, suggestions, solutions, and three or four easily reproducible activity sheets.

House, Peggy, ed. *Providing Opportunities for the Mathematically Gifted, K–12.* National Council of Teachers of Mathematics, 1987.

Ideas are based on the premise that the mathematically gifted are a virtually untapped resource who have not been stimulated to reach their full potential.

Huntley, H. E. *The Divine Proportion: A Study in Mathematical Beauty.* Dover, 1970.

Some of the topics treated are patterns, Fibonacci numbers, Pascal's triangle, golden numbers, and the divine proportion.

Jacobs, Harold. *Mathematics, A Human Endeavor.* W. H. Freeman, 1994.

Many mathematics topics explored in a creative and surprising manner.

Katz, Victor J. *History of Mathematics: An Introduction.* 2nd ed. Addison Wesley Longman, 1998.

King, James, and Doris Schattschneider, eds. *Geometry Turned On.* Mathematical Association of America, 1997.

This reference promotes use of dynamic geometry, that is, active, exploratory geometry carried out with interactive computer software in the study and teaching of geometry. Dynamic geometry is an indispensable tool to investigate geometry constructions and design for projects and research.

Klee, Victor, and Stan Wagon. *Old and New Unsolved Problems in Plane Geometry and Number Theory.* Mathematical Association of America, 1991.

Twenty-four central problems placed in a historical and mathematical context. Many of the problems are accompanied by other, related problems.

Kline, Morris. *Mathematics: The Loss of Certainty.* Oxford, 1982.

A history of the relationship between mathematics and science and of the development of the philosophy and foundations of mathematics from antiquity to the present; requires some mathematical maturity, but nicely written.

Landwehr, James M., and Anne E. Watkins. *Exploring Data.* Dale Seymour, 1994.

Students are challenged to analyze data using tables, mean, median, smoothing, scatter plots, stem-and-leaf plots, box plots, and other techniques (grades 7–10).

Landwehr, James M., Jim Swift, and Ann E. Watkins. *Exploring Surveys and Information from Samples.* Dale Seymour, 1986.

Students learn the basics of statistical inference by studying sample opinion polls, such as the Gallup. Simulation replaces complicated formulas to develop confidence intervals. The text considers random sampling and practical aspects of drawing samples to minimize bias and error (grades 10–12).

Lappan, Glenda, James T. Fey, William M. Fitzgerald, Susan N. Friel, and Elizabeth Phillips. *The Connected Mathematics Project.* Dale Seymour, 1997–98.

A standards-based middle school mathematics curriculum funded by NSF that incorporates projects, scoring guides, and modeling in all units.

MCTM/SIMMS Integrated Mathematics: A Modeling Approach Using Technology. Levels 1, 2, 3, 4, 5, & 6 (SE and TE). Simon & Schuster Custom Publishing, 1996–98.

An NCTM *Standards*-based curriculum that incorporates real-world contexts. Each of the six levels of materials for grades 9–12 involves algebra, geometry, trigonometry, analysis, statistics, probability, and data analysis. Also less traditional high school topics such as graph theory, game theory, and chaos theory are encountered. Technology is an integral part of the curriculum as are explorations and projects.

National Council of Teachers of Mathematics. *Learning and Teaching Geometry, K–12.* 1987 Yearbook of the National Council of Teachers of Mathematics, edited by Mary Montgomery Lindquist. National Council of Teachers of Mathematics, 1987.

Geometry depicted in problem solving and its applications; activities; blending geometry with other areas of mathematics; how students learn geometry including van Hiele levels.

————. *Problem Solving in School Mathematics.* 1980 Yearbook, edited by Stephen Krulik. National Council of Teachers of Mathematics, 1980.

————.*The Teaching and Learning of Algorithms in School Mathematics.* 1998 Yearbook, edited by Lorna J. Morrow. Reston, Va.: National Council of Teachers of Mathematics., 1998.

Addresses questions about algorithms, their relevance, and their use in school mathematics at all levels.

Ore, Oystein (revised and updated by Robin J. Wilson). *Graphs and Their Uses.* Mathematical Association of America, 1990.

An excellent introduction to the field of graph theory. New material is included on interval graphs, the traveling salesman problem, bracing frameworks, shortest-route problems, and coloring maps on surfaces.

Parker, Sybil P., ed. *McGraw-Hill Dictionary of Mathematics*. McGraw Hill, 1997

Perl, Teri. *Math Equals: Biographies of Women Mathematicians and Related Activities*. Addison Wesley Longman, 1978.

Discusses the personal lives and work of nine famous female mathematicians who overcame obstacles to make significant contributions.

Polya, George. *Mathematical Discovery: On Understanding, Learning, and Teaching Problem Solving*. John Wiley & Sons, 1981.

The author is a master at leading readers to guess answers and to discover mathematics.

Posamentier, Alfred S., and Wolfgang Schulz. *The Art of Problem Solving: A Resource for Mathematics Teachers*. Corwin Press, 1996.

Mathematics professionals from all over the world bring you their best strategies. Twenty chapters of attention-grabbers ranging from practical to theoretical, from common to glitzy.

Reid, Constance. *From Zero to Infinity*. Mathematical Association of America, 1992.

This book shows how interesting the everyday natural numbers, 1, 2, 3, ... have been for over two thousand years and still are today. It combines the mathematics and history of number theory with descriptions of the mystique that has, on occasion, surrounded numbers.

Rosenstein, Joseph G., Deborah S. Franzblau, and Fred S. Roberts, eds. *Discrete Mathematics in the Schools*. American Mathematical Society, 1997.

This volume, a collection of articles by experienced educators, explains why and how, including evidence for why and practical guidance for how. It also discusses how discrete mathematics can be used as a vehicle for achieving the broader goals of the major effort now under way to improve mathematics education.

Sadovskií, L. E., and A. L. Sadovskií. *Mathematical World Series: Mathematics and Sports*. American Mathematical Society, 1993.

A nice survey of applications of mathematics in sporting events.

Sobel, Max A., ed. *Readings for Enrichment in Secondary School Mathematics*. National Council of Teachers of Mathematics, 1988.

A collection of articles previously printed in several NCTM sources; it also contains three original chapters on harmonic mean, rotation matrices and complex numbers, and how computers and calculators perform arithmetic.

Solow, Daniel. *How to Read and Do Proofs: An Introduction to Mathematical Thought Processes*. John Wiley & Sons, 1982.

Specific techniques for beginning and writing proofs: one of the few books devoted to the topic of writing proofs.

Spencer, Donald D. *Spencer's Illustrated Computer Dictionary*. 3rd. ed. Camelot, 1995.

A sourcebook for high school or college students interested in computer science, computer literacy, and data processing.

Staszkow, Ronald. *The Math Palette*. 2nd ed. Saunders, 1995.

> This relevant and enjoyable book for liberal arts majors teaches mathematics through discovery annd application. Topics illustrate the evolution and practicality of mathematics.

Steen, Lynn Arthur, ed. *On the Shoulders of Giants: New Approaches to Numeracy*. Washington, D.C.: National Academy Press, 1990.

> What mathematics should be learned by today's young people and tomorrow's workforce? This book is a vision of the richness of mathematics expressed in essays on change, dimension, quantity, shape and uncertainty. These essays expand on the idea of mathematics as the language and science of patterns.

Straffin, Philip D., Jr., ed. *Applications of Calculus*. Mathematical Association of America, 1993.

> Readers see how calculus can explain the structure of a rainbow, guide a robot arm, or analyze the spread of AIDS. Each module starts with a concrete problem and moves on to provide a solution.

Thomas, David. *Active Geometry*. Brooks/Cole, 1998.

> Students investigate a wide variety of geometrical topics in search of powerful relationships and concepts. The activities provide motivation for students, leading them to construct, observe, conjecture, and debate their thinking.

Periodicals

Periodicals that should be available for use by students include the following:

American Mathematical Monthly. Mathematical Association of America (MAA).

> Although this is a college-level magazine, it is a valuable source of ideas and problems.

Teaching Children Mathematics. National Council of Teachers of Mathematics (NCTM).

> Directed toward content and pedagogy in grades K–4; titled *Arithmetic Teacher* until May 1994.

The College Mathematics Journal. Mathematical Association of America.

> Titled *The Two-Year College Mathematics Journal* until 1983; mathematics articles appropriate for the upper high school through college mathematics levels.

Journal of Computers in Mathematics and Science Teaching. Association for Advancement of Computing in Education.

Mathematics Magazine. Mathematical Association of America.

> A college-level magazine that is a source of problems and suggestions.

Mathematics Teacher. National Council of Teachers of Mathematics.

> This journal is directed toward the content and pedagogy of mathematics in grades 9–12.

Teaching Mathematics in the Middle School. National Council of Teachers of Mathematics.

> This journal is directed toward the content and pedagogy of mathematics in grades 5–8.

Scientific American. Scientific American.

Every issue devotes space to mathematics. It has served as a fertile source for mathematics projects in the past.

School Science and Mathematics. School Science and Mathematics Association (SSMA).

Problems for high school students are included in this magazine. Applications of mathematics to science may be found here also.

Student Math Notes. National Council of Teachers of Mathematics.

Lessons on different mathematical topics for students in grades K–12. This is included in the *NCTM News Bulletin.*

Articles and Book Chapters

The suggestions, comments, and ideas in the following articles are worthwhile for anyone interested in mathematics projects, mathematics fairs, or mathematics clubs.

Bruckheimer, Maxim, and Rina Hershkowitz. "Mathematics Projects in Junior High School." *Mathematics Teacher* 70 (October 1977): 573–78.

Dalton, LeRoy C. "A Student-Presented Mathematics Club Program—Non-Euclidean Geometries." *Mathematics Teacher* 73 (September 1980): 450–51.

Draper, Roni Jo. "Active Learning in Mathematics: Desktop Teaching." *Mathematics Teacher* 90 (November 1997): 622–25.

McConnell, John W. "Forging Links with Projects in Mathematics." In *Connecting Mathematics across the Curriculum.* 1995 Yearbook of the National Council of Teachers of Mathematics, edited by Peggy A. House, pp. 198–209. Reston, Va.: National Council of Teachers of Mathematics, 1995.

Morgan, Frank, Edward R. Melnick, and Ramona Nicholson. "The Soap Bubble Geometry Contest." *Mathematics Teacher* 90 (December 1997): 746–49.

PUBLISHERS: NAMES AND ADDRESSES

Academic

Academic Press
6277 Sea Harbor Dr.
Orlando, FL 32887
(800) 321-5068
www.academicpress.com

Activity Resources

Activity Resources Company
(Distributed by Cuisenaire)
P.O. Box 4875
20655 Hathaway Ave.
Hayward, CA 94541
(510) 782-1300

Addison Wesley Longman

Addison Wesley Longman
1 Jacob Way
Reading, MA 01867
(617) 944-3700
(800) 447-2226
www2.awl.com/corp

American Mathematical Society

American Mathematical Society
P.O. Box 6248
Providence, RI 02940
(800) 321-4267
(401) 455-4000
fax: (401) 331-3842
ams@ams.org

Basil Blackwell
Blackwell Publishers
238 Main St.
Cambridge, MA 02142
(800) 216-2522

Birkhauser
(Division of Springer-Verlag)
Birkhauser Boston
675 Massachusetts Ave.
Cambridge, MA 02139
info@birkhauser.com

Brooks/Cole
(Div. of International Thompson
   Pub. Ed. Group)
Brooks/Cole Publishing Co.
511 Forest Lodge Rd.
Pacific Grove, CA 93950
(408) 373-0728

Carolina Biological Supply
Carolina Biological Supply Co.,
Publications Department
2700 York Rd.
Burlington, NC 27215
(800) 334-5551

Cambridge
Cambridge University Press
40 W. 20th St.
New York, NY 10011
(800) 221-4512
www.cup.cam.ac.uk/

Camelot
Camelot Publishing Co.
P.O. Box 1357
Ormond Beach, FL 32175-1357
(904) 672-5672

CBS
CBS Educational and Professional
   Publishing
383 Madison Ave.
New York, NY 10017

Chapman & Hall
Chapman & Hall
(Division of Routledge, Chapman &
   Hall)
115 5th Ave., 4th Floor
New York, NY 10003-1004

Corwin Press
(Subs. of Sage Publishing)
Corwin Press, Inc.
2455 Teller Rd.
Thousand Oaks, CA 91320-2218

Cuisenaire
(Subs. of Addison Wesley Longman)
Cuisenaire Co. of America, Inc.
P.O. Box 5026
White Plains, NY 10602-5026

Dover
Dover Publications
31 E. 2nd St.
Mineola, NY 11501
(516) 294-7000

Everyday Learning Corporation
(Bought Janson Publishing)
2 Prudential Plaza
Suite 1200
Chicago, IL 60601
(800) 382-7670
elccsr@tribune.com

Franklin Watts
Franklin Watts Inc.
387 Park Ave., S.
New York, NY 10016

Freeman
W. H. Freeman & Co.
41 Madison Ave.
New York, NY 10010
(212) 576-9400

Greenwood
(Imprint of Greenwood Publishing
   Group)
Greenwood Press
88 Post Rd. W., Box 5007
Westport, CT 06881
(203) 226-3571
(800) 225-5800 (orders only)

Hafner
(Div. of Macmillan Publishing Co.)
Macmillan Publishing Co.
100 Front St. Box 500
Riverside, NJ 08075-7500
(609) 461-6500

HarperCollins
(Subsidiary of News Corp., Ltd.)
HarperCollins Publishers, Inc.
10 East 53rd St.
New York, NY 10022-5299
(800) 331-3761

Houghton Mifflin
Houghton Mifflin Co.
222 Berkely St.
Boston, MA 02116
(800) 225-3362

IEEE
IEEE Computer Society Press
10662 Los Vaqueros Cir.
Los Alamitos, CA 90720
(800) 272-6657

ITP
International Thompson Pub.
7625 Florence Dr.
Empire, KY 41042
(800) 282-5700

Johns Hopkins
Johns Hopkins University Press
2715 N. Charles St.
Baltimore, MD 21218-4319
(800) 537-5487

Key Curriculum Press
Key Curriculum Press
P.O. Box 2304
Berkeley, CA 94702
(800) 995-6284

Little, Brown
(A Time Warner Company)
Little, Brown & Co.
Time & Life Bldg.
1271 Ave. of the Americas
New York, NY 10020
(800) 343-9204

Mathematical Association of America
Mathematical Association of
America
P.O. Box 91112
Washington, DC 20090-1112
(800) 331-1622

Macmillan
Macmillan Publishing Co., Inc.
200 Old Tappan Road
Old Tappan, NJ 07675
(800) 223-2336
www.macmillan.com

McDougal Littell
P.O. Box 1667
Evanston, IL 60204

McGraw
McGraw-Hill Book Co.
1221 Ave. of the Americas
New York, NY 10020
(800) 262-4729
www.mcgraw-hill.com

MSU—Bozeman
Montana State University—Bozeman
MSU Bookstore
Strand Union
MSU—Bozeman
Bozeman, MT 59717
(406) 994-2811

Mu Alpha Theta
601 Elm Ave., Room 423
Norman, OK 73019
(405) 325-4489

NCTM
National Council of Teachers of
   Mathematics
1906 Association Dr.
Reston, VA 20191-1593
(800) 235-7566
nctm@nctm.org

**New York City Board of
Education**
131 Livingston St., Room 613
Brooklyn, NY 11201

Norton
W. W. Norton & Co.
500 5th Ave.
New York, NY 10110
(800) 223-2584

Oxford
Oxford University Press
198 Madison Ave.
New York, NY 10016-4314
(800) 451-7556
www.oup-usa.org

Paul & Co. Pubs.
Paul & Company Publishers
   Consortium, Inc.
COSI
2 Christie Heights St.
Leonia, NJ 06705
(210) 840-4700

Plenum Press
(Imprint of Plenum Publishing
   Corp.)
233 Spring St.
New York, NY 10013-1578

Prentice-Hall
Prentice-Hall, Inc.
1 Lake St.
Upper Saddle River, NJ 07458-1813
(201) 909-6200
www.prenhall.com

Princeton
Princeton University Press
41 William St.
Princeton, NJ 08540
(800) 777-4726

Prindle, Weber & Schmidt
Prindle, Weber & Schmidt
20 Park Plaza
Boston, MA 02116-4501

Random
Random House
201 E. 50th St., 22nd Floor
New York, NY 10022
(800) 726-0600
www.randomhouse.com

Saint Martin's
St. Martin's Press
175 5th Ave., Room 1715
New York, NY 10010
(800) 221-7945

Saunders
(Subs. of Harcourt Brace & Co.)
Saunders College Publishing
Public Ledger Building
150 Independence Mall West
Suite 1250
Philadelphia, PA 19105-3412
(215) 238-5500

Dale Seymour
(Subs. of Addison Wesley Longman)
Dale Seymour Publications
200 Middlefield Rd.
Menlo Park, CA 94025
(800) 872-1100

Simon

Simon & Schuster Custom
  Publishing
Route 59 & Brookhill Dr.
West Nyack, NY 10994
(208) 332-6800

Springer-Verlag

Springer-Verlag New York, Inc.
175 5th Ave.
New York, NY 10010
(800) 777-4643
www.springer.de

TAB Books

(Division of McGraw-Hill)
TAB Books
13311 Monterey Lane
Blue Ridge Summit, PA 17294-0850

Texas Instruments

Texas Instruments, Inc.
P.O. Box 655303-8345
Dallas, TX 75265
(214) 997-6412

University Press

University Press
6521 California St.
San Francisco, CA 94121
(415) 731-1702

Viking Penguin

Viking Penguin
375 Hudson St.
New York, NY 10014-3657
(800) 331-4624

Waveland

Waveland Press
P.O. Box 400
Prospect Heights, IL 60070
(708) 634-0081

Wide World Publishing

Wide World Publishing/Tetra
P.O. Box 476
San Carlos, CA 94070
(415) 593-2839

Wiley

John Wiley & Sons
605 3rd Ave.
New York, NY 10158
(908) 469-4400

PERIODICALS: NAMES AND ADDRESSES

College Mathematics Journal
(formerly the *Two-Year College
Mathematics Journal*)
Mathematics Magazine
Mathematics Monthly

Mathematical Association of
America
1529 18th St., NW
Washington, DC 20036
(202) 387-5250
ums@ams.org

*Journal of Computers in
Mathematics and Science Teaching*

Association for Advancement of
Computing in Education
P.O. Box 2966
Charlottesville, VA 22902
(804) 973-3987
aace@virginia.edu

Mathematics Teaching in the Middle School

Mathematics Teacher

Teaching Children Mathematics
(Formerly *Arithmetic Teacher*)

National Council of Teachers of
Mathematics
1906 Association Dr.
Reston, VA 20191-1593
(703) 620-9840
nctm@nctm.org

School Science and Mathematics

School Science and Mathematics
    Association
Weniger Hall 237
Oregon State University
Corvallis, OR 97331
(541) 737-1818
pratt@bloomu.edu

Scientific American

Scientific American
415 Madison Ave.
New York, NY 10017
(212) 754-0550
reprints@sciam.com

Note: The NCTM Regional
Services Committee has a list of
various NCTM Affiliate Groups
that publish journals.

5

References

BOOKS AND PAMPHLETS

1. Abbott, Edwin A. *Flatland.* HarperCollins Publishers, 1983.
2. Agostini, Franco. *Math and Logic Games.* Seymour, 1986.
3. Albers, Donald, and Gerald L. Alexanderson. *Mathematical People: Profiles and Interviews.* Birkhauser, 1986.
4. Albers, Donald J., Gerald L. Alexanderson, and Constance Reid, eds. *More Mathematical People: Contemporary Conversation.* Academic, 1994.
5. Anderson, Marlow. *A First Course In Abstract Algebra.* Prindle, Weber & Schmidt, 1995.
6. Armstrong, Mark Anthony. *Basic Topology.* Springer-Verlag, 1997.
7. Austin, Joe Dan, ed. *Applications of Secondary School Mathematics.* National Council of Teachers of Mathematics, 1981.
8. Banchoff, Thomas F. *Beyond the Third Dimension: Geometry, Computer Graphics, and Higher Dimensions.* Mathematical Association of America, 1996.
9. Beckman, Peter. *A History of Pi.* Dale Seymour, 1971.
10. Bendick, Jeanne. *How Much and How Many?* Franklin Watts, 1989.
11. Bennett, Dan, William Finzer, Greer Lleud, Joan Meyers, and Steven Rasmussen, eds. *The Geometer's Sketchpad: User Guide and Reference Manual.* Key Curriculum, 1995.
12. Bezuszka, Stanley, Margaret J. Kenney, and Stephen M. Kokoska. *Applications of Mathematics through Models and Formulas.* Dale Seymour, 1987.
13. Billstein, Rick, and Jim Williamson. *MathThematics, Books 1, 2, & 3 (SE and TE).* McDougal Littell, 1999.
14. Brualdi, Richard A. *Introductory Combinatorics,* 3rd ed. Prentice-Hall, 1997.
15. Brueningsen, Chris, and Elisa William. *Explorations: Exploring Math on the TI-92, What Is the Number "e"?* Texas Instruments, 1996.
16. Burns, Marilyn. *This Book Is about Time.* Little, Brown & Co., 1978.
17. Burrill, Gail, John C. Burrill, Pamela Coffield, Gretchen Davis, Jan de Lange, Diann Resnick, and Murray Siegel. *Data Analysis and Statistics across the Curriculum.* Addenda Series, Grades 9–12. National Council of Teachers of Mathematics, 1992.
18. Burrill, Gail, M. Clifford, Patrick Hopfensperger, R. Scheaffer, and Jeffrey Witmer. *Data Driven Mathematics Series.* Dale Seymour, 1997.
19. Campbell, Douglas, and John Higgins. *Mathematics: People, Problems, Results.* Vols. 1, 2, & 3. Chapman & Hall, 1984.

20. Chhatwal, G. R. *History of Mathematics and Computer Science.* State Mutual Book and Periodical Services, 1995.

21. Cohen, Marcus, Edward D. Gaughan, Arthur Knoebel, Douglas S. Kurtz, and David Pengelley. *Student Research Projects in Calculus.* Mathematical Association of America, 1992.

22. Cooney, Mariam, ed. *Celebrating Women in Mathematics and Science.* National Council of Teachers of Mathematics, 1996.

23. Copes, Lawrence E. *Investigating Algebra: A Novel Approach to Abstract Algebra.* Addison Wesley Longman, 1998.

24. Courant, Richard, Herbert Robbins, and Ian Stewart. *What Is Mathematics?: An Elementary Approach to Ideas and Methods,* 2nd ed. New York: Oxford, 1996.

25. Couthron, Julia H., Ronald N. Giese, and Richard J. Rezba. *Students and Research: Practical Strategies for Science Classrooms and Competitions.* 2nd ed. Kendall/Hunt Publishing Company, 1993.

26. Coxford, Arthur F., Jr., Linda Burks, Claudia Giamati, and Joyce Jonik. *Geometry From Multiple Perspectives.* Addenda Series, Grades 9–12. National Council of Teachers of Mathematics, 1991.

27. Crisler, Nancy, Patience Fisher, and Gary Froelich. *Discrete Mathematics through Applications.* W. H. Freeman, 1994.

28. Dalton, Leroy C., and Henry C. Snyder, eds. *Topics for Mathematics Clubs.* 2nd ed. National Council of Teachers of Mathematics, 1983.

29. Datta, Biswa N. *Numerical Linear Algebra and Applications.* Brooks/Cole, 1998.

30. Demana, Franklin, Gregory Foley, Bert K. Waits, and Stanley Clemens. *Precalculus: Functions and Graphs.* 3rd ed. Addison Wesley Longman, 1997.

31. DeMeulemeester, Katie. *Math Projects: Organization, Implementation, and Assessment.* Dale Seymour, 1995.

32. Devaney, Robert. *Chaos, Fractals, Dynamics: Computer Experiences in Mathematics.* Addison Wesley Longman, 1989.

33. Devlin, Keith. *Mathematics: The Science of Patterns.* W. H. Freeman & Co., 1997.

34. Ernst, Bruno. *Adventures with Impossible Figures.* New York: Parkwest Publications, 1987.

35. Esty, Warren W. *The Language of Mathematics.* Montana State University—Bozeman, 1998.

36. Faires, J. Douglas, and Richard Burden. *Numerical Methods.* 2nd ed. Brooks/Cole, 1998.

37. Farmer, David W. *Groups and Symmetry: A Guide to Discovering Mathematics.* American Mathematical Society, 1996.

38. Farmer, David W., and Theodore B. Stanford. *Knots and Surfaces: A Guide to Discovering Mathematics.* American Mathematical Society, 1996.

39. Fauvel, John, and Jeremy Gray. *The History of Mathematics: A Reader.* Macmillan, 1996.

40. Field, Michael, and Martin Golubitsky. *Symmetry in Chaos: A Search for Pattern in Mathematics, Art and Nature.* Oxford, 1996.

41. Finney, Ross L., George B. Thomas, Jr., Bert K. Waits, and Franklin D. Demana. *Calculus: A Graphing Approach.* Addison Wesley Longman, 1993.

42. Fitzgerald, William, Susan N. Friel, and Elizabeth D. Phillips. *Thinking with Mathematical Models.* Connected Mathematics. Dale Seymour, 1998.

43. Fletcher, Peter, and C. Wayne Patty. *Foundations of Higher Mathematics.* Prindle, Weber & Schmidt, 1996.

44. Gardner, Martin. *Mathematical Carnival.* Washington, D.C.: Mathematical Association of America, 1989.

45. ———. *Penrose Tiles to Trapdoor Ciphers.* Freeman, 1989.

46. ———. *Penrose Tiles to Trapdoor Ciphers … and the Return of Dr. Matrix.* Mathematical Association of America, 1997.

47. Garland, Trudi. *Fascinating Fibonaccis: Mystery and Magic in Numbers.* Dale Seymour, 1988.

48. ———. *Math and Music: Harmonious Connections.* Cuisenaire/Dale Seymour, 1994.

49. Geddes, Dorothy, Julianna Bove, Irene Fortunato, David J. Fuys, Jessica Morgenstern, and Rosamond Welchman-Tischler. *Geometry in the Middle Grades.* Addenda Series, Grades 5–8. National Council of Teachers of Mathematics, 1992.

50. Gerver, Robert. *Writing Math Research Papers.* Key Curriculum Press, 1997.

51. Gnanadesikan, Mirudulla, Richard L. Scheaffer, and Jim Swift. *The Art and Techniques of Simulation.* Dale Seymour, 1994.

52. Goodwan, Frederick M. *Introduction to Abstract Algebra.* Prentice-Hall, 1997.

53. Green, Thomas M., and Charles L. Hamberg. *Pascal's Triangle.* Dale Seymour, 1986.

54. Grinstein, Louise S., and Paul J. Campbell, eds. *Women of Mathematics: A Biobibliographic Sourcebook* Greenwood, 1987.

55. Gullberg, Jan. *Mathematics: From the Birth of Numbers.* Norton, 1997.

56. Guy, Richard K. *Unsolved Problems in Number Theory.* Springer-Verlag, 1995.

57. Haeussler, Ernest F., and Richard S. Paul. *Introductory Mathematical Analysis for Business, Economics, and the Life and Social Sciences.* 7th ed. Prentice-Hall, 1993.

58. Heid, M. Kathleen, Jonathan Choate, Charlene Sheets, and Rose Mary Zbiek. *Algebra in a Technological World.* Addenda Series, Grades 9–12. National Council of Teachers of Mathematics, 1995.

59. Henderson, Linda Dalrymple. *The Fourth Dimension and Non-Euclidean Geometry in Modern Art.* Princeton, 1983.

60. Henry, Boyd. *Explorations in Mathematics for the Secondary Student.* Everyday Learning, 1994.

61. Hilton, Peter, and Jean Pedersen. *Build Your Own Polyhedra.* Addison Wesley Longman, 1988.

62. Hirsch, Christian R., and Robert A. Laing, eds. *Activities for Active Learning and Teaching: Selections from the "Mathematics Teacher."* National Council of Teachers of Mathematics, 1993.

63. Hoenig, Alan. *Applied Finite Mathematics.* Houghton Mifflin, 1995.

64. Hopper, Clarence. *Visualizing Calculus: Powerful Programs for Graphing Calculators.* Dale Seymour, 1997.

65. House, Peggy, ed. *Providing Opportunities for the Mathematically Gifted, K–12.* National Council of Teachers of Mathematics, 1987.

66. Houston, S. Ken, Werner Blum, Ian Huntley, and N. T. Neill. *Teaching and Learning Mathematical Modeling: Innovation, Investigation and Applications.* Paul & Co. Pubs, 1997.

67. Hughes-Hallett, Deborah. *Calculus: Single Variable.* 2nd ed. John Wiley & Sons, 1997.

68. Hughes-Hallett, Deborah, Andrew M. Gleason, eds. *Applied Calculus.* John Wiley & Sons, 1994.

69. Huntley, H. E. *The Divine Proportion: A Study in Mathematical Beauty.* Dover, 1970.

70. Jackson, Brad. *Applied Combinatorics with Problem Solving.* 2nd ed. Addison Wesley Longman, 1998.

71. Jacobs, Harold. *Mathematics, A Human Endeavor.* Freeman, 1994.

72. Johnson, Donovan A. *Paper Folding for the Mathematics Class.* National Council of Teachers of Mathematics, 1995.

73. Jones, Graham A., et al. *Algebra, Data and Probability Explorations for Middle School: A Graphics Calculator Approach.* Dale Seymour, 1997.

74. Katz, Victor J. *History of Mathematics: An Introduction.* 2nd ed. Addison Wesley Longman, 1998.

75. Kenney, Margaret J., ed. *Discrete Mathematics across the Curriculum, K–12.* 1991 Yearbook of the National Council of Teachers of Mathematics. National Council of Teachers of Mathematics, 1991.

76. Kincaid, David and Ward Cheney. *Numerical Analysis: Mathematics of Scientific Computing.* Brooks/Cole, 1996.

77. King, James, and Doris Schattschneider, eds. *Geometry Turned On.* Mathematical Association of America, 1997.

78. Klee, Victor, and Stan Wagon. *Old and New Unsolved Problems in Plane Geometry and Number Theory.* Mathematical Association of America, 1991.

79. Kline, Morris. *Mathematics: The Loss of Certainty.* Oxford, 1982.

80. Knauff, Robert E. *Short Stories from the History of Mathematics.* Carolina Biological, 1996.

81. Krause, Eugene F. *Taxi-Cab Geometry.* Dover, 1986.

82. Landwehr, James M., and Ann E. Watkins. *Exploring Data.* Dale Seymour, 1994.

83. Landwehr, James M., Jim Swift, and Ann E. Watkins. *Exploring Surveys and Information from Samples.* Dale Seymour, 1986.

84. Lappan, Glenda, James T. Fey, William M. Fitzgerald, Susan N. Friel, and Elizabeth Difanis Phillips. *The Connected Mathematics Project.* Dale Seymour, 1997–98.

85. Larson, Rolan. *Brief Calculus with Applications.* 4th ed. Houghton-Mifflin, 1995.

86. Laycock, Mary. *Straw Polyhedra.* Activity Resources, 1992.

87. Long, Calvin T. *Elementary Introduction to Number Theory.* 3rd ed. Waveland, 1995.

88. Lovitt, Charles, and Ian Lowe. *Chance and Data Investigations: Volumes 1 and 2.* Victoria, Australia: Curriculum Corporation, 1994.

89. Lyng, Merwin. *Dancing Curves: A Dynamic Demonstration of Geometric Principles.* National Council of Teachers of Mathematics, 1978.

90. *MCTM/SIMMS Integrated Mathematics: A Modeling Approach Using Technology. Levels 1, 2, 3, 4, 5, & 6 (SE and TE).* Simon & Schuster Custom Publishing, 1996–98.

91. McKim, Robert. *Thinking Visually.* Dale Seymour, 1990.

92. Moise, Edwin. *Elementary Geometry from an Advanced Standpoint.* Addison Wesley Longman, 1990.

93. Nakamura, Shoichiro. Numerical Analysis and Graphic Visualization with MATLAB. Prentice-Hall, 1995.

94. National Council of Teachers of Mathematics. *Applications in School Mathematics.* 1979 Yearbook of the National Council of Teachers of Mathematics, edited by Sidney Sharron. National Council of Teachers of Mathematics, 1979.

95. ———. *The Ideas of Algebra, K–12.* 1988 Yearbook of the National Council of Teachers of Mathematics, edited by Arthur F. Coxford. National Council of Teachers of Mathematics, 1988.

96. ———. *Learning and Teaching Geometry, K–12.* 1987 Yearbook of the National Council of Teachers of Mathematics, edited by Mary Montgomery Lindquist. National Council of Teachers of Mathematics, 1987.

97. ———. *Problem Solving in School Mathematics.* 1980 Yearbook of the National Council of Teachers of Mathematics, edited by Stephen Krulik. National Council of Teachers of Mathematics, 1980.

98. ———. *The Teaching and Learning of Algorithms in School Mathematics.* 1998 Yearbook of the National Council of Teachers of Mathematics, edited by Lorna J. Morrow. National Council of Teachers of Mathematics, 1998.

99. Newman, Claire M., Thomas E. Obremski, and Richard L. Scheaffer. *Exploring Probability.* Dale Seymour, 1986.

100. Newman, M. H. *Elements of the Topology of Plane Sets of Points.* Dover, 1992.

101. Ore, Oystein. *Graphs and Their Uses.* Revised by Robin J. Wilson. Mathematical Association of America, 1990.

102. Pappas, Theoni. *The Joy of Mathematics: Discovering Mathematics All around You.* Wide World Publishing, 1989.

103. ———. *Mathematical Scandals.* Wide World Publishing, 1997.

104. Parker, Sybil P., ed. *McGraw-Hill Dictionary of Mathematics.* McGraw-Hill, 1997.

105. Peitgen, Heinz-Otto, Hartmut Jurgens, and Dietmar Saupe. *Fractals for the Classroom (Part One: Introduction to Fractals and Chaos; Part Two: Complex Systems and Mandelbrot Set).* Springer-Verlag. 1992.

106. Perl, Teri. *Math Equals: Biographies of Women Mathematicians and Related Activities.* Addison Wesley Longman, 1978.

107. Phillips, Elizabeth, Theodore Gardella, Constance Kelley, and Jacqueline Stewart. *Patterns and Functions.* Addenda Series, Grades 5–8. National Council of Teachers of Mathematics, 1991.

108. Phillips, G. M., and P. J. Taylor. *Theory and Applications of Numerical Analysis.* 2nd ed. Academic Press, 1996.

109. Pohl, Victoria. *How to Enrich Geometry Using String Designs.* National Council of Teachers of Mathematics, 1986.

110. Polya, George. *Mathematical Discovery: On Understanding, Learning, and Teaching Problem Solving.* John Wiley & Sons, 1981.

111. Posamentier, Alfred S. *Excursions in Advanced Euclidean Geometry.* Dale Seymour, 1984.

112. Posamentier, Alfred S., and Wolfgang Schulz. *The Art of Problem Solving: A Resource for Mathematics Teachers.* Corwin, 1996.

113. Posamentier, Alfred S., and William Wemick. *Advanced Geometric Constructions.* Dale Seymour, 1988.

114. Prasolov, V. V. *Intuitive Topology.* American Mathematical Society, 1994.

115. Reid, Constance. *From Zero to Infinity.* Mathematical Association of America, 1992.

116. Rosenstein, Joseph G., Deborah S. Franzblau, Fred S. Roberts, eds. *Discrete Mathematics in the Schools.* American Mathematical Society and National Council of Teachers of Mathematics, 1997.

117. Rossman, Allan J. and J. Barr Von Oehsen. *Workshop Statistics: Discovery with Data and the Graphing Calculator.* Springer-Verlag, 1997.

118. Ryan, Patrick J. *Euclidean and Non-Euclidean Geometry: An Analytic Approach.* Cambridge, 1986.

119. Sachs, Leroy C., ed. *Projects to Enrich School Mathematics, Level 3.* 2nd ed. National Council of Teachers of Mathematics, 1988.

120. Sadovskií, L. E., and A. L. Sadovskií. *Mathematical World Series: Mathematics and Sports.* Washington, D.C.: American Mathematical Society and National Council of Teachers of Mathematics, 1993.

121. Sagan, Carl. *Billions and Billions: Thoughts on Life and Death on the Brink of the Millennium.* Random House, 1997.

122. Seymour, Dale. *Encyclopedia of Math Topics and References. A Resource for Projects and Explorations.* Dale Seymour, 1995.

123. ———. *Introduction to Line Designs.* Dale Seymour, 1992.

124. ———. *Introduction to Tessellations.* Dale Seymour, 1986.

125. ———. *Geometric Design.* Dale Seymour, 1988.

126. ———. *Visual Patterns in Pascal's Triangle.* Dale Seymour. 1986

127. Seymour, Dale, and M. Shedd. *Finite Differences (8–12).* Dale Seymour, 1979.

128. Sharp, Richard. *The Sneaky Square & 113 Other Math Activities for Kids.* TAB Books, 1990.

129. Scheaffer, Richard L., M. Gnanadesikan, A. Watkins, and J. A.Witmer. *Activity-Based Statistics.* Springer-Verlag, 1997.

130. Shifrin, Theodore. *Abstract Algebra: A Geometric Approach.* Prentice-Hall, 1995.

131. Sierra, Michael. *Patty Paper Geometry.* Dale Seymour, 1998.

132. Smart, James R. *Modern Geometries.* 5th ed. Brooks/Cole, 1997.

133. Smart, Margaret. *Excursions In Geometry for Middle School.* Activity Resources, 1994.

134. Sobel, Max A., ed. *Readings for Enrichment in Secondary School Mathematics.* National Council of Teachers of Mathematics, 1988.

135. Souviney, R., M. Britt, S. Gargiulo, and P. Hughes. *Mathematical Investigations.* Dale Seymour, 1990.

136. Solow, Daniel. *How to Read and Do Proofs: An Introduction to Mathematical Thought Processes.* John Wiley & Sons, 1982.

137. Spencer, Donald D. *Exploring Number Theory with Microcomputers.* 3rd ed. Camelot, 1995.

138. ———. *Spencer's Illustrated Computer Dictionary.* 3rd ed. Camelot, 1995.

139. ———. *The Timetable of Mathematics: A Chronology of the Most Important People and Events in the History of Mathematics.* Camelot, 1998.

140. Staszkow, Ronald. *The Math Palette.* 2nd ed. Saunders, 1995.

141. Steen, Lynn Arthur, ed. *On the Shoulders of Giants: New Approaches to Numeracy.* Western Academy Press. 1990.

142. Stein, Dorothy. *Ada, a Life and a Legacy.* Cambridge, 1985.

143. Stewart, Ian. *Game, Set, and Math: Enigmas and Conundrums.* Basil Blackwell, 1989.

144. Stewart, James. *Calculus: Concepts and Contexts.* International Thompson Publications, 1998.

145. Straffin, Philip D., Jr., ed. *Applications of Calculus.* Mathematical Association of America, 1993.

146. Swetz, Frank, and Jefferson S. Hartzler, eds. *Mathematical Modeling in the Secondary School Curriculum: A Resource Guide of Classroom Exercises.* National Council of Teachers of Mathematics, 1991.

147. Thomas, David. *Active Geometry.* Brooks/Cole, 1998.

148. Townsend, M. Stewart. *Mathematics in Sport.* Prentice-Hall, 1984.

149. Tucker, Alan. *Applied Combinatorics.* 3rd ed. John Wiley & Sons, 1994.

150. vosSavant, Marilyn. *The World's Most Famous Math Problem: The Proof of Fermat's Last Theorem and Other Mathematical Mysteries.* Saint Martin's, 1993.

151. Wahl, Bernt. *Exploring Fractals on the Macintosh (9 and up).* Dale Seymour, 1995.

152. Weaver, Jefferson Hane. *Conquering Statistics: Numbers without the Crunch.* Plenum Press, 1997.

153. Wells, David. *The Penguin Dictionary of Curious and Interesting Numbers.* Viking Penguin, 1998.

154. Wenninger, Magnus J. *Polyhedron Models.* Cambridge, 1974.

155. Whatley, Sherron. *Creative Line and String Design.* Activity Resources, 1996.

156. Wicks, John R. *Linear Algebra with Mathematica.* Addison Wesley Longman, 1996.

157. Williams, David E. *Mathematics Teacher's Complete Calculator Handbook.* Prentice-Hall, 1984.

158. Williams, Michael R. *A History of Computing Technology.* IEEE Computer Society, 1997.

159. Wolfram, Stephen. *The Mathematica Book.* Cambridge, 1996.

160. Woodward, Ernest, and Thomas Hamel. *Geometric Constructions and Investigations with a Mira ™.* Dale Seymour, 1992.

161. Zawojewski, Judith, et al. *Dealing with Data and Chance.* Addenda Series: Grades 5–8. National Council of Teachers of Mathematics, 1991.

ARTICLES

162. Andreasen, Corey. "Fibonacci and Pascal Together Again: Pattern Exploration in the Fibonacci Sequence." *Mathematics Teacher* 91 (March 1998): 250–53.

163. Arcavi, Abraham. "Using Historical Materials in the Math Classroom." *Arithmetic Teacher* 35 (December 1987): 13–16.

164. Austin, Richard A., and Denisse R. Thompson. "Exploring Algebraic Patterns through Literature." *Mathematics Teaching in the Middle School* 2 (February 1997): 274–81.

165. Barnes, Sue, and Karen Dee Michalowicz. "Now and Then: From Königsberg to Columbus." *Mathematics Teaching in the Middle School* 1 (September–October 1995): 460–65.

166. Bennett, Betsy. "Now and Then: Ann Wagner, Mechanical Engineer." *Mathematics Teaching in the Middle School* 2 (September–October 1996): 22–29.

167. ———. "Now and Then: Counting on the Air." *Mathematics Teaching in the Middle School* 1 (January–February 1996): 630–36.

168. Bidwell, J. K. "Using Reflections to Find Symmetric and Asymmetric Patterns." *Arithmetic Teacher* 34 (March 1987): 10–15.

169. Bradie, Brian. "Rate of Change of Exponential Functions: A Precalculus Perspective." *Mathematics Teacher* 91 (March 1998): 224–37.

170. Brieske, Tom. "Visual Thinking with Translations, Halfturns, and Dilations." *Mathematics Teacher* 77 (September 1984): 466–69.

171. Bruckheimer, Maxim, and Rina Hershkowitz. "Mathematics Projects in Junior High School." *Mathematics Teacher* 70 (October 1977): 573–78.

172. Burk, Frank. "Some Interesting Consequences of a Hyperbolic Inequality." *College Mathematics Journal* 17 (January 1986): 75–76.

173. Casey, James. "Perfect and Not-So-Perfect Rollers." *Mathematics Teacher* 91 (January 1998): 12–20.

174. Coes, Loring III. "More Functions of a Toy Balloon." *Mathematics Teacher* 90 (April 1997): 290–302.

175. Cuff, Carolyn K. "The Binomial Theorem Tastes the Rainbow." *Mathematics Teacher* 91 (March 1998): 262–64.

176. Curcio, Fran, Barbara Nimerofsky, Rossana Perez, and Shirel Yoloz. "Exploring Patterns in Nonroutine Problems." *Mathematics Teaching in the Middle School* 2 (February 1997): 262–69.

177. Dalton, LeRoy C. "A Student-Presented Mathematics Club Program— Non-Euclidean Geometries." *Mathematics Teacher* 73 (September 1980): 450–52.

178. Draper, Roni Jo. "Active Learning in Mathematics: Desktop Teaching." *Mathematics Teacher* 90 (November 1997): 622–25.

179. Dugdale, Susan. "Newton's Method for Square Root: A Spreadsheet Investigation and Extension into Chaos." *Mathematics Teacher* 91 (October 1998): 576–85.

180. Durkin, Marilyn B., and Barbara C. Nevils. "Using Spreadsheets to See Chaos." *Journal of Computers in Mathematics and Science Teaching* 13 (1994): 321–38.

181. Fragale, Kendra C. "The Case of Jewels Jones." *Mathematics Teaching in the Middle School* 1 (November-December 1995): 584–88.

182. Frantz, Marny, and Sylvia Lazarnick. "Data Analysis and the Hardrock 100." *Mathematics Teacher* 90 (April 1997): 274–76.

183. Good, Robert C., Jr. "The Binary Abacus: A Useful Tool for Explaining Computer Operations." *Journal of Computers in Mathematics and Science Teaching* 5 (Fall 1985): 34–37.

184. Gorman, Jacqueline. "Strategy Games: Treasures from Ancient Times." *Mathematics Teaching in the Middle School* 3 (October 1997): 110–16.

185. Greeley, Nansee, and Theresa Reardon Offerman. "Now and Then: Measuring Angles in Physical Therapy." *Mathematics Teaching in the Middle School* 2 (March-April 1997): 338–46.

186. Haak, Sheila. "Using the Monochord: A Classroom Demonstration on the Mathematics of Musical Scales." *Mathematics Teacher* 75 (March 1982): 238–44.

187. Hess, Adrien L. "Viewing Diagrams in Four Dimensions." *Mathematics Teacher* 64 (March 1971): 247–48.

188. Hoffman, Dale T. "Smart Soap Bubbles Can Do Calculus." *Mathematics Teacher* 72 (May 1979): 377–85, 389.

189. Holden, Lyman S., and Loyce K. Holden. "Tacoma Shuffle." *Mathematics Teacher* 91 (March 1998): 212–16.

190. Horak, Virginia M., and Willis J. Horak. "Geometric Proofs of Algebraic Identities." *Mathematics Teacher* 74 (March 1981): 212–16.

191. Hughes, Barnabas, and Kim A. Anderson. "American and Canadian Indians—Mathematical Connectors." *Mathematics Teaching in the Middle School* 2 (November-December 1996): 80–83.

192. Johnson, Art, and Joan D. Martin. "The Secret of Anamorphic Art." *Mathematics Teacher* 91 (January 1998): 24–32.

193. Johnson, Iris DeLoach. "Paving the Way to Algebraic Thought Using Residue Designs." *Mathematics Teacher* 91 (April 1998): 326–32.

194. Johnson, Luella H. "A Look at Parabolas with a Graphing Calculator." *Mathematics Teacher* 90 (April 1997): 278–82.

195. Johnson, Millie. "Exploring Graphs: WYSIWYG." *Mathematics Teaching in the Middle School* 2 (March-April 1997): 328–31.

196. Kader, Gary D., and Mike Perry. "Pennies from Heaven—Nickels from Where?" *Mathematics Teaching in the Middle School* 3 (November-December 1997): 240–48.

197. Karp, Karen S., and Robert N. Ronau. "Birthdays and the Binary System: A Magical Mixture." *Mathematics Teaching in the Middle School* 3 (September 1997): 6–12.

198. Kimberling, Clark. "Microcomputer-Assisted Discoveries: Euclidean Algorithm and Continued Fractions." *Mathematics Teacher* 76 (October 1983): 510–12, 548.

199. Kliman, Marchlene, and Susan Janssen. "Translating Number Words into the Language of Mathematics." *Mathematics Teaching in the Middle School* 1 (May 1996): 798–800.

200. Lamb, John F. "Two Egyptian Construction Tools." *Mathematics Teacher* 86 (February 1993): 166–67.

201. Lauber, Murray. "Casting Out Nines: An Explanation and Extensions." *Mathematics Teacher* 83 (November 1990): 661–65.

202. Lemon, Patricia. "Pascal's Triangle-Patterns, Paths and Plinko." *Mathematics Teacher* 90 (April 1997): 270–73.

203. Lovinelli, Robert. "Using Spreadsheets to Analyze Historical Perspectives of Apportionment." *Mathematics Teacher* 91 (February 1998): 176–82.

204. McClintock, Ruth M. "The Pyramid Question: A Problem Solving Adventure." *Mathematics Teacher* 90 (April 1997): 262–68.

205. McConnell, John. "Forging Links with Projects in Mathematics." In *Connecting Mathematics across the Curriculum*, 1995 Yearbook of the National Council of Teachers of Mathematics, edited by Peggy A. House, pp. 198–209. National Council of Teachers of Mathematics, 1995.

206. McGehee, Jean J. "Interactive Technology and Classic Geometry Problems." *Mathematics Teacher* 91 (March 1998): 204–8.

207. Malloy, Carol E. "Mathematics Projects Promote Students' Algebraic Thinking." *Mathematics Teaching in the Middle School* 2 (February 1997): 282–88.

208. Manuel, George, and Amalia Santiago. "An Unexpected Appearance of the Golden Ratio." *College Mathematics Journal* 19 (March 1988): 168–70.

209. May, E. Lee. "Are Seven-Game Baseball Playoffs Fairer?" *Mathematics Teacher* 85 (October 1992): 528–31.

210. Markowitz, Lee. "Area = Perimeter." *Mathematics Teacher* 74 (March 1981): 222–23.

211. Michalowicz, Karen Dee. "Fractions of Ancient Egypt in the Contemporary Classroom." *Mathematics Teaching in the Middle School* 1 (May 1996): 786–89.

212. Millman, Richard, and Romona Speranza. "The Artist's View of Points and Lines." *Mathematics Teacher* 84 (February 1991): 133–38.

213. Morgan, Frank, Edward R. Melnick and Ramona Nicholson. "The Soap Bubble Geometry Contest." *Mathematics Teacher* 90 (December 1997): 746–49.

214. Naraine, Bishnu, and Emam Hoosain. "Investigating Polygonal Regions: Making Conjectures and Proving Theorems." *Mathematics Teacher* 91 (February 1998): 135–40.

215. Nord, Gail, and John Nord. "Sediment in Lake Coeur d'Alene, Idaho." *Mathematics Teacher* 91 (April 1998): 292–96.

216. Patterson, Anne. "Building Algebraic Expressions: A Physical Model." *Mathematics Teaching in the Middle School* 2 (February 1997): 238–42.

217. Perry, M., and Gary Kader. "Counting Penguins." *Mathematics Teacher* 91 (February 1998): 110–16.

218. Poggi, Jeanlee M. "An Invitation to Topology." *Arithmetic Teacher* 33 (December 1985): 8–11.

219. Pollack, Paul. "My Application of the Pythagorean Theorem." *Mathematics Teaching in the Middle School* 1 (May 1996): 814–16.

220. Provost, Fernand J. "The Conic Sections in Taxicab Geometry: Some Investigations for the High School Student." *Mathematics Teacher* 91 (April 1998):. 304–7, 341.

221. Quesada, Antonio R. "Recent Improvements to the Sieve of Eratosthenes." *Mathematics Teacher* 90. (April 1997): 304–7.

222. Rector, Robert E. "Game Theory: An Application of Probability." *Mathematics Teacher* 80 (February 1987): 138–42.

223. Rubenstein, Rheta. "The Function Game." *Mathematics Teaching in the Middle School* 2 (November-December 1996): 74–78.

224. Salisbury, Andrew John. "Some Strategies Games Using Desargue's Theorem." *Mathematics Teacher* 75 (November 1982): 652–53.

225. Schimmel, Judith. "A New Spin on Volumes of Solids of Revolution." *Mathematics Teacher* 90 (December 1997): 715–17.

226. Schwartzman, Steven. "Factoring Polynomials and Fibonacci." *Mathematics Teacher* 79 (January 1986): 54–56, 65.

227. Shilgalis, Thomas W. "Finding Buried Treasures—an Application of the Geometer's Sketchpad." *Mathematics Teacher* 91 (February 1998): 162–65.

228. Shirley, Lawrence. "Activities from African Calendar and Time Customs." *Mathematics Teaching in the Middle School* 1 (January-February 1996): 616–20.

229. Simmt, Elaine, and Brent Davis. "Fractal Cards: A Space for Exploration in Geometry and Discrete Mathematics." *Mathematics Teacher* 91 (February 1998): 102–8.

230. Slavit, David. "Above and Beyond AAA: The Similarity and Congruence of Polygons." *Mathematics Teaching in the Middle School* 3 (January 1998): 276–80.

231. Stacey, Kaye, and Mollie MacGregor. "Building Foundations for Algebra." *Mathematics Teaching in the Middle School* 2 (February 1997): 252–60.

232. St. John, Dennis. "Exploring Hill Ciphers with Graphing Calculators." *Mathematics Teacher* 91 (March 1998): 240–44.

233. Uccellini, John C. "Teaching the Man Meaningfully." *Mathematics Teaching in the Middle School* 2 (November-December 1996): 112–15.

234. VanLeuvan, Patricia. "Young Women Experience Mathematics at Work in the Health Professions." *Mathematics Teaching in the Middle School* 3 (November-December 1997): 198–206.

235. Vonder Embse, Charles V., and Vernon W. Yoder. "Multiple Representations and Connections Using Technology." *Mathematics Teacher* 91 (January 1998): 62–67.

236. Walton, Karen Doyle. "Albert Durer's Renaissance Connections between Mathematics and Art." *Mathematics Teacher* 87(April 1994): 278–82.

237. Wiener, Joseph. "Bernoulli's Inequality and the Number *e*." *College Mathematics Journal* 16 (November 1985): 399–400.

238. Wilson, Melvin R. (Skip), and Carol M. Krapfl. "Exploring Mean, Median, and Mode with a Spreadsheet." *Mathematics Teaching in the Middle School* 1 (September-October 1995): 490–95.

Software

239. Cabri Geometry, Texas Instruments

240. Geometer's Sketchpad, Key Curriculum Press

241. Geometric superSupposer, Sunburst Publications

242. TesselMania!, Dale Seymour Publications

Appendix A
Evaluation CRITERIA (Form 2)

Project Title _____

Project Creator _____

High → Low

DISPLAY

project is logically presented and easy to read   4   3   2   1

display is visually appealing (including lettering
and colors)   4   3   2   1

data is shown clearly in tables, charts, or pictures
with headings   4   3   2   1

project clearly explains what the student learned   4   3   2   1

project represents study and effort   4   3   2   1

results or conclusion are shown clearly   4   3   2   1

INTERVIEW

student clearly communicated how the problem was solved   4   3   2   1

student clearly communicated the conclusion   4   3   2   1

student clearly communicated extensions   4   3   2   1

student spoke freely and confidently   4   3   2   1

student answered questions clearly   4   3   2   1

PAPER

attention is shown to detail; neat   4   3   2   1

attention is paid to grammar and spelling   4   3   2   1

tables, graphs, and diagrams are detailed and labeled   4   3   2   1

visuals are attractive and informative   4   3   2   1

conclusions summarize results with specific details   4   3   2   1

methodology for collecting data is described   4   3   2   1

procedure is clearly explained   4   3   2   1

published information is correctly cited   4   3   2   1

Comments:

Appendix B

LIST OF MATHEMATICIANS AND STATISTICIANS BY SUBJECT AREA

Geometry

Euclid, Fibonacci, Descartes, Fermat, Agnesi, Khayyam, Thales, Pythagoras, Archimedes, Pascal, Euler, Gauss, Einstein, daVinci, Kepler, Appolonius

Algebra

Khayyam, Fibonacci, Descartes, Agnesi, Somerville, Abel, Einstein, Hypatia, Newton, Galois, Noether, Muhammad ibn Musa, Boole

Number Systems and Number Theory

Euclid, Fibonacci, Fermat, Abel, Pythagoras, Archimedes, Pascal, Lagrange, Germain, Gauss, Galois, Ramanujan, Leibniz, Eratosthenes, Cardano, Young

Probability

Cardano, Fermat, Pascal, Bernoulli, Rutherford, Fisher, Chebyshev

Computation and Estimation

Archimedes, Napier, Pascal, Gauss, Ramanujan

Calculators and Computers

Babbage, Lovelace, Hopper

Fractals

Mandelbrot, vonKoch, Sierpinski, Menger, Peano, Hilbert

Calculus

Agnesi, Kovalevsky, Jakob Bernoulli, Johann Bernoulli, Kepler, Newton, Leibniz, Germain, duChatelet, Young, Taussky-Todd

Women in Mathematics

Agnesi, Somerville, Lovelace, Hypatia, Germain, Noether, Kovalevsky, Hopper, duChatelet, Rudin

Statistics

Neyman, Pearson, vonNeumann, Tukey

Topology

Möbius, Euler, Klein, Jordan, Rudin

Appendix C

TIMELINES AND RESPONSIBILITIES

Planning and using a timeline of work is one of the many learning experiences a long-range project helps students achieve. The successful student finds this to be a valuable lifelong skill. When long-range projects are assigned to students, it is important to include and inform parents or guardians periodically throughout the project. Adults need to understand their role and that of the mentor's in the project. It is tempting for well-meaning parents to want to do the project for the student. Suggestions for adult roles should be addressed in the initial communications. (See Appendix D.) Also included should be information describing the project, its goals, timeline, and if possible, sample rubrics or scoring guides. It's a good idea to have parents as well as the teacher and student sign off on the pivotal dates in the timeline. This should encourage parents to help the student with the planning process and avoid the last minute panic that inevitably sets in the night before the project is due. Adults who are not related to the student can often be valuable role models. Including the community in educational endeavors can be an added benefit.

Each student should have a file with timeline, sign-off sheets, rough drafts and plans, and any other pertinent information kept in the classroom. This helps the student and teacher organize the many facets of individual and group projects.

If community members are asked to participate in evaluating the projects, it is important that they understand the guidelines the students were given. If possible, a teacher or other adult who has been heavily involved with the project should meet with the evaluators prior to the presentations for a short briefing on what to look for and how scores should be awarded. It can be very disheartening to students to work hard on a long-term project only to have it judged harshly because the evaluator did not understand the criteria.

A project can be a worthwhile experience for students of any age if they are properly prepared all along the way. It is important not to assume they are capable of this type of planning. Helping them be prepared is a large part of the adults'—teacher or mentor—job.

Timeline—Two-Month Project

Week 1

- Brainstorm ideas in class. Use list as beginning point.
- Produce a list of two or three possible project ideas.
- Discuss the criteria for judging. (See Appendix A and chapter 1.)
- Alert parents to expect a letter of explanation (see Appendix D).

Week 2

- State the title of the project and a brief statement of intent.
- Encourage students to find a mentor in the community.

Week 3

- Submit a research progress update.

Week 4

- Submit a research progress update.

Week 5

- Submit a research progress update.

Week 6

- Submit a research progress update.
- Produce a first draft of the paper. (See chapter 1.)
- Create a first draft sketch of the πproject display.

Week 7

- Produce a second draft of the paper.
- Produce a final sketch of the project display.
- Produce a final draft of the paper.

Week 8

- Set up a display of the project for classmates.
- Practice interviewing with classmates.
- Set up a working display for evaluators and the public.
- Participate in the Mathematics Fair event at the end of the week.

Follow-up

- Dissemination Possibilities:
  Present the project to local service groups or district classrooms.
  Write an article for a newsletter or journal.
  Interview with the local newspaper.
  Publish an article in the school paper.

To the Student

Keep a record of your thoughts and ideas, even work that does not seem to lead to a correct answer. A failed method for one aspect of a problem may well be the key to another aspect. A notebook that is dedicated to these thoughts and ideas will be extremely helpful as you are working. It is very important that you spend a sufficient amount of time thinking about your project.

MATH PROJECT—WORKING FORM

Name:

Date due	Date done	Week 1: Possible Topics
		1
		2
		3.
		Week 2: Topic Statement
		Draft title of project
		Brief Statement of Intent
		Community mentor Name Occupation, work address, phone number, e-mail address Expertise related to project

www.math.montana.edu/~star/NCTMProjectBook

Date due	Date done	**Week 3:** Research Update
		Information found and research conducted
		Week 4: Research Update
		Information found and research conducted
		Week 5: Research Update
		Information found and research conducted
		Week 6: Research Update
		Information found and research conducted
		Paper—First Draft Turn in first draft of paper. Include books, articles, and interviews in the bibliography.
		Sketch of Project Display Turn in first draft sketch of project presentation A trifold paper will be helpful when visualizing the working model.

Date due	Date done	**Week 7:** Paper—Second Draft
		Turn in the draft with revisions. Include list of people who helped with editing.
		Paper—Final Draft Final draft due with cover sheet
		Sketch of Project Display—Final Draft Sketch includes sizes of diagrams, pictures, color of letters, background, and so on.
		Week 8: Paper and Project—Class Presentation
		Set up in exhibit area. Be prepared for questions from classmates.
		Interview Practice interviewing with classmates. Create a list of questions that you are prepared to answer.
		Set Up for Judging Have the project set up and be prepared to answer questions at ____. time
		Participate in the Mathematics Fair Event
		Week 9: Plan for Dissemination
		When and where will you be making presentations?

Appendix D

<Date>

Dear Parent or Guardian,

This term your student will be participating in a mathematics project of her or his choosing. The purpose of the project is to give students the opportunity to apply their understanding of mathematics to situations of personal interest. Many times this will be an interdisciplinary project with links to other areas such as science, technology, music, sports, or art. The project may also explore deeper connections within the field of mathematics.

This is also an opportunity for you to share in your child's learning and work cooperatively with an inspiring teacher. Studies have shown that children's interests in science and mathematics are strongly influenced by their guardians or parents. When families enthusiastically participate in the prospect of studying a topic in depth, stimulating conversations can occur, and all participants can learn.

Even though your interest, support, and enthusiasm are critical components of your student's success, it is important to remember that the project should be the student's work. Please be generous with both your encouragement and constructive criticism as the occasion warrants.

Here are some strategies you can use throughout the course of the project to make the process a successful experience:

- Help your student adhere to the timeline for project deadlines that has been developed by the teacher.

- Show continued interest, and express support.

- Frequently ask for an informal progress report.

- Offer to provide the proper tools, materials, and an adequate workspace.

- Provide transportation to meetings with your student's mentor, teacher, or student group.

- Encourage your child to practice a formal presentation or interview with you or the family.

I am excited about providing this opportunity for extending your child's mathematical understanding in ways that are meaningful. If you have any questions or concerns at any time during the project, please feel free to call me at <phone number>.

Sincerely,

<teacher's name>

Appendix E

ACCESSING INTERNET RESOURCES

Assume that you want to search for information concerning discrete mathematics through articles published by NCTM in the *Mathematics Teacher* journal.

- Obtain access to a computer with a software search engine such as Netscape, Yahoo, Metacrawler, or Excite at a public library, school, or at home.

- Type in the address www.nctm.org. Another approach is to use search software to find the National Council of Teachers of Mathematics by working through general categories such as Mathematics or Education. NCTM can be referenced from Web site home pages of many organizations. If NCTM lettering is in a color other than black, use the mouse and cursor to click on NCTM. You will be taken directly to the NCTM Web site.

- From the NCTM home page, a succession of alternatives are provided:

Move cursor to word(s) and click mouse	Address that appears
publications	www.nctm.org/publications
Mathematics Teacher	www.nctm.org/mt/mt.htm
search	www.nctm.org/mt/mt-search.htm

Enter the words "discrete mathematics" (including the quotation marks), and press return to obtain a list of *Mathematics Teacher* articles related to discrete mathematics. Once you know correct addresses, use your Internet software to type in the address and proceed directly to that location, bypassing intermediate steps. Use a software feature called "bookmarks" to save and access regularly used Web site addresses easily. Others may be written in this handbook in boxes underneath the appropriate topic. Since Web sites are frequently created or eliminated, it is important to update your references.